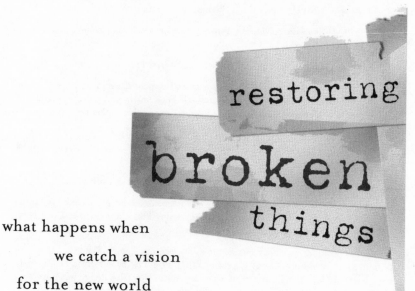

restoring
broken
things

what happens when
we catch a vision
for the new world
Jesus is creating

Steven Curtis Chapman
Scotty Smith

INTEGRITY®
PUBLISHERS
Nashville

Library of Congress Cataloging-in-Publication Data

Chapman, Steven Curtis.
Restoring broken things : what happens when we catch a vision for the new world Jesus is creating / by Steven Curtis Chapman and Scotty Smith.
p. cm.
Summary: "Practical implications of Jesus' commitment to make all things new and the part we are to play with Him in this redemptive process"—Provided by publisher.

ISBN 1-59145-280-5 (harcover)

1. Reconciliation—Religious aspects—Christianity. 2. Christian life. 3. Redemption—Christianity. 4. Jesus Christ. I. Smith, Scotty, 1950– II. Title.
BT738.27.C43   2005
234'.4 dc22   2005008311

I dedicate this book to Emily, Caleb, Will,
Shaohannah, Stevey, Maria, and Mary Beth.

—Steven Curtis Chapman

With great joy, I dedicate this book to my compassionate
and courageous wife, Darlene,
and our awesome children and their spouses,
Kristin and Ran, and Scott and Bayley.
Thanks for tantalizing my heart with images
and the aroma of the newness Jesus is
bringing to all things.

—Scotty Smith

CONTENTS

Foreword		vii
Acknowledgments		xi
Prologue	Broken Beyond Repair	xiii
Chapter 1	The Restorer of Broken Things	1
Chapter 2	The Importance of Story	15
Chapter 3	Engaging with God's Story of Restoration	33
Chapter 4	Understanding Brokenness	55
Chapter 5	Restoring God's Broken Creation	77
Chapter 6	Restoring Broken Lives	97
Chapter 7	Restoring Broken Relationships	117
Chapter 8	Restoring Broken Worship	137
Chapter 9	Restoring Broken Worshipers	157
Chapter 10	Restoring God's Broken Church	181
Chapter 11	Restoring Broken Culture	209
Conclusion	What on Earth Are We Doing?	231
Endnotes		253

FOREWORD

I didn't want to read this book. I love Scotty and have long respected Steven Curtis Chapman. But when I was asked to read this book and offer a few thoughts for an introduction, I didn't think much about *needing* what they wrote. I was wrong.

My labor is primarily with men and women who have experienced the dark, broken heartache of sexual abuse. As the president of Mars Hill Graduate School, I aim to engage the hearts of men and women courageous enough to enter the darkness and brokenness of their own lives—in order to eventually sing a new-creation song. Many of our students know the fault lines of abuse; they all know the heartache of living in a fallen world. So how could I not know?

Despite being submerged in others' brokenness, I somehow forgot my own. Yet God allowed me to experience new death and new life during the same season I read *Restoring Broken Things*.

My wife and I recently lost a friendship with a couple who are divorcing. The story is common: A wife has accused her husband of an affair. The husband denies it and says that his wife has been insanely jealous and acting bizarre for years. She says he is a liar; he says she is crazy. Each friend requires us to agree with them if we wish to remain friends. We don't know who is telling the truth, or even if it really matters. We know that we love both husband and wife, yet the decision not to choose sides broke fellowship with both of them.

Of course, other friends chose sides and know for certain which spouse is at fault. As a result, these friends have since called us traitors to some degree or another. The fallout involves a wide web of family, friends, and acquaintances—and it seems as if the sorrow will never end. A dear friend who went to work in Sri Lanka after the tsunami compares it to removing layer upon layer of debris—only to find a new horror under each collapsed wall. No wonder we'd rather hide the dead and offer slogans of hope that ignore the sorrow.

As I read the book, I found tears rolling down my face as I considered the brokenness of my life and my world. I was enticed to read both by the profound honesty and the sweet fragrance of life that caught my senses from its first pages. Death is the pretext for resurrection. Resurrection is the context in which we more honestly name the extent of our brokenness. There simply can be no joy without deeply facing the sorrow of death.

Chapter by chapter, I was invited to rest in the inexplicable kindness of God. I was drawn to the arms of love that offer solace to those who refuse to settle for anything less than a broken and contrite heart. If it is the kindness of God that leads to repentance, then we can't find healing for our brokenness until we are broken in heart and overwhelmed by the kindness of God.

It dawned on me why I didn't want to read *Restoring Broken Things*. I'm not merely afraid of more pain or the struggle of living in a fallen world. I'm afraid to allow myself to hope. What if chaos and loss are really all there is to life? When life becomes more clearly broken, it is almost harder to hope than simply endure. With brilliance and tenderness, Scotty and Steven Curtis chronicle the wild and glorious way that God redeems brokenness and transforms ashes into beauty. I have never been so tenderly drawn to the Cross.

A few weeks ago brought reconciliation with an old friend whom I have been estranged from for more than six years. Our relationship was broken due to another friend's accusation and gossip. Years ago, we attempted to reconcile, but it only seemed to add more brokenness. We each tried to speak words of repentance and forgiveness, but there was no sweetness of reconciliation or wonder in dancing together at the feast for prodigals. It was a right thing to do, but it lacked life and joy.

More years passed and a sudden and surprising day came when I sat with my friend in the lobby of a hotel. While hundreds of other conference speakers and attendees were milling about, we wept tears of sweet, inconceivable joy. My friend and I sat and spoke of our sorrow and desire to be friends again.

We each named our failure of love in the past, but it was simply not the issue. Something greater than our sin and brokenness had dawned, and in the light of a new, lovely day, there was kindness and care. A river of tears flowed before the God who will plant not one tree of life by the river of joy, but a whole orchard.

Six years was an eternity to wait. But the moment glory rises it is like the passing of labor pains as one holds the newborn child. To experience the power of reconciliation is to look at brokenness and know it will not win. Darkness will not suffocate the light.

Am I willing to wait, hope, and labor for reconciliation with our friends who are divorcing? With the reminder of this book and the transforming power of a hope-filled God, yes.

Restoring Broken Things will take you on a journey of hope that will enable you to step more honestly into the heartache and more richly into the joy offered by our resurrected God. It will help you remember there is nothing worth living for but the promise of restoration.

—Dan B. Allender, Ph.D.
President, Mars Hill Graduate School

ACKNOWLEDGMENTS

(STEVEN:)

Thanks to Joey, Byron, Angela, and the entire team at Integrity Publishers; Dan, David, Jeanie, Jim, and everyone at Creative Trust; Bill, Peter, Brad, and everyone at EMI CMG; John and my friends at CAA; my band and road crew; David, Melissa, and Grace. Thanks also to Scott at Shaohannah's Hope and its many supporters for their sacrifices serving children in need of a forever family. Special thanks to Scotty Smith, my co-author, pastor, and friend—I'm grateful to you for mentoring me and for the message of this book, which inspired so much of the album *All Things New*. Thanks for doing this with me.

(SCOTTY):

Many thanks and kudos to the Integrity Publishers family—especially Byron, Joey, and Angela—for making my first writing project with them such a joy. And special thanks to Marcus Yoars, for making the difficult process of editing such an utter delight. As always, my assistant, Sue McCallum, brought the WD40 of God's grace to the writing process during my always-crazy life and schedule. Lastly, thanks to my dear friend, Steven Curtis, for a decade and a half of friendship and partnership in God's Big Story of redeeming love.

PROLOGUE:
BROKEN BEYOND REPAIR

(STEVEN:)

Nervous wondering gave way to immediate bonding the first time my wife and I laid eyes on our seven-month-old bundle of grace. Every hour we held Shaohannah added sixty more minutes of disbelief to the realization that this tiny image-bearer of God was found abandoned along a path when she was just a few days old.

Though Shaoey had been in our hearts for months, she'd only been placed in our arms forty-eight hours earlier at the Grand Sun City Hotel in Changsha, China, where the adoption was finalized. With our commitment to become adoptive parents also came a promise to give our daughter as much of *her* story and culture as possible. That's why we wouldn't take Shaoey to her new home in Tennessee until we first visited the only home she'd ever known.

Ever since the first day she was rescued and brought to an orphanage near the village of Changde, in the Hunan Province,

Shaoey had been well loved. And we wanted to see, touch, and enter this part of her story for ourselves.

"Steven and Mary Beth, right this way . . . here we are. *This* is where your daughter slept." Surrounded by the sights and sounds of so many other precious children filling the room, we approached this space with great respect. We were thirsty to experience as much of the first months of her life as we could, and we drank in every square inch of Shaoey's vacant bed—with its little blanket folded neatly at one end of the crib and the now nameless name cardholder.

Like being caught in an unexpected downpour, I wasn't prepared for the burst of emotions that welled up inside of me as these simple elements took on enormous symbolic meaning. Two images came to mind, one right after the other. Not exactly like a song lyric, but just as real, the thought came to me: "One bed at a time . . . *that's* how we've *got* to think about the daunting challenge of caring for so many orphans. One bed at a time."

Just a few days earlier, our family had stood in Tiananmen Square, in downtown Beijing, staggered by the sheer numbers of people swarming about and saddened by the hovering sense of heaviness and the glaring absence of joy and laughter. It was like walking into an IMAX movie of hopelessness.

Now, holding Shaoey, encircled by many children with stories just as heartbreaking as hers . . . well, it's hard to know *what* to do when you feel like you're standing before an ocean of need with just a teaspoon to help. Are some things *broken beyond repair*? There's no way we can be sure, but estimates of the number of orphaned children in China range between one and twenty million—and that's just in *China*.

The quiet whisper of God's Spirit is the only voice that could've given me some sense of perspective during that dizzying moment. I found myself thinking, *Jesus is not expecting any of us to put our arms around the* whole *orphan crisis . . . but we can fill our arms and empty an orphanage, one bed at a time . . . one bed at a time.* In our family story, that has led to two more empty beds in China and two more sisters for Emily, Will, Caleb and Shaoey . . . Stevey Joy and Maria.

But it was the second image that assured me this quiet sense of hope was anchored to God's heart and not merely my attempt to manage difficult emotions in the presence of a seemingly impossible situation. Shaoey's empty bed and folded blanket made me think about another emptied resting place and folded cloth: *Jesus' tomb on Easter morning!*

The *only* basis for any real and lasting hope—about *anything*—is that Jesus died for our sins on the Cross, was buried in a tomb, and was raised from the dead on the third day, inaugurating the greatest restoration project imaginable. Jesus has promised to make *all things new*, and He has also given us His word that He will return one day to *completely* rid the world of *every* expression and evidence of death and sin—including the deaths and sin that leave millions of children as orphans and those that enable us to mute their cries by our indifference, fear, selfishness, and excuses.

Jesus' resurrection is the reason why our "little" labors in the Lord are not in vain. What on earth is Jesus doing? How is He "restoring broken things" in the face of the insurmountable needs of the world? *One* bed in *one* orphanage at a time. One person, clueless about the gospel, at a time. One tsunami victim at a time. One AIDS patient at a time. One elderly neighbor at a time. One abused wife at a time. One poor, foodless family at a time.

Warning: Work in Progress

(Scotty:)

Welcome to a story that is still very much a work in progress. You'll notice that the title of our book is *Restoring Broken Things*, not *Things Already Restored*. Steven and I are quick to count ourselves among the many broken things that Jesus is in the *process* of making new. We readily take our place in the inglorious family portrait of God's people captured in the Bible. It's a picture framed in grace—a *motion* picture with grace appearing in every frame, for there is nothing static or stationary about God's Story. His is the story from which all other stories derive their meaning, and like all great stories, it has a beginning, middle, and an end.

God's Story has a certain redundancy to it. His family is consistently revealed as Cinderella with amnesia, Frodo with cataracts, and Robinson Crusoe with ADD. We forget our privileged identity, lose sight of our amazing destiny, and wander into all kinds of self-defeating calamity.

More importantly, this Story has a *most certain redemption* to it. By documenting the failings and foibles of His children, God has made His Story all the more authentic, beautiful, and believable. Much more significantly, He has magnified the glory and grace of His Son, Jesus, who by His life, death, and resurrection has secured a never-ending ending to God's Story—an ending more wonderful than anything we could ask or imagine. This book is committed to surveying and savoring this *certain redemption* and its *magnificent fruition.*

We offer this book as a collection—a montage of stories, studies, snapshots, songs, and scenes from the one big Story that God is telling in the Bible of His redeeming and restoring love in Jesus. It's our prayer that you will find your place in this bigger story. Not all of us are called to become adoptive parents, but every one of us *is* called to be the means—in many different ways—by which it will become evident to people all around us that Jesus has come to make all things new.

1 THE RESTORER OF BROKEN THINGS

"Behold, I am making all things new."
—REVELATION 21:5

"You make all things new . . . You make all things new
You redeem and You transform . . .
You renew and You restore
You make all things new . . .
and forever we will watch and worship You"
— SCC, "All Things New"

(SCOTTY):

The Art House was electric with anticipation. Nestling down into my chair, I took a few minutes to gather myself and prepare for the much-ballyhooed afternoon event—a pre-release viewing of Mel Gibson's movie, *The Passion of the Christ.* Charlie Peacock and his wife, Andi, welcomed about forty of us into their lovely home to see and discuss an uncut version of the controversial film. Steven was out of town, but Mary Beth ably represented the Chapman family. We were asked to give Mel Gibson our feedback *face-to-face*, as the famous actor was present. Needless to say, all of us felt honored to be included in such an experience.

1

But honored wasn't the primary thing I was feeling that Thursday afternoon—try emotional exhaustion. At the time, so many people I cared about were dealing with great loss, need, and pain. I knew the answer, but I still needed to voice the question: "Is anything *not* broken in the world?" Sometimes hope emerges when you least expect it.

BROKEN FAMILIES

It'd been a week since I returned from visiting my dad in North Carolina—a trip that left a sweet and sour residue in my heart. The sweet: I've never been as close to my dad as I am right now. We're five short years into knowing each in a way that will make one of us weep bitterly when he buries the other. Gone are the days of our three-topic, five-minute conversations: "How's work? Can you believe the taxes we're paying? Getting to play any golf?" I never dreamed there'd be a day when we'd sit together comfortably and talk about anything, with neither of us checking our watches. I had more faith that the whole city of Nashville would come to Christ than the possibility of my dad and I ever physically embracing and connecting emotionally.

The sour: A threat to this precious gift is looming on the horizon. That sharp mind—exercised daily for decades in the gymnasium of navigating calculations, and then by crossword puzzles and six o'clock *Jeopardy* in retirement—is losing its edge. How many of you have had one of your parents look you straight in the eyes and momentarily forget you are his or her child? I have, and it hurts. How I thank God for the past few years of rich relationship with Dad. But when will momentary become permanent?

2

BROKEN SOCIETIES

On Monday, three days before viewing *The Passion*, I received confirmation of the specific dates for my next mission trip to South Africa, Ethiopia, and Kenya. Now that the flights were booked, it didn't take twenty-four hours for the emotional wattage generated on my *last* trip to Africa to become current. Messy and inconvenient feelings were waking from a comfort-induced slumber.

The helplessness of holding an HIV-positive baby in a hospice nursery just outside of Cape Town; the alien joy of Christians lining up to care for, and adopt, the growing multitude of AIDS orphans; the witch doctor who, having asked us to pray for a sick woman, covered her ears as we invoked the name of Jesus; the repulsive smell of poverty and hunger hovering over the slums of Nairobi, and the even *more* repugnant stench of red tape, payola, and scams that divert money—given for the poor—into the pockets of corrupt government officials. All these images were begging for fresh attention.

BROKEN CHURCHES AND PASTORS

Nothing whine-worthy happened on Tuesday, but Wednesday reminded me why the thought of winning the lottery and retiring from pastoring occasionally looks pretty good. The familiar red folder stared up at me from the corner of my assistant's desk. This folder contains a number of things that require my signature: notes to our visitors from the previous Sunday, baptism certificates, letters of transfer for members either entering or leaving our church family, minutes from elders' meetings, and other personal correspondence.

This particular day, there were only letters from our members wishing to transfer their membership to three different churches, all within a five-mile radius of our facility. Now I've been a pastor long enough to anticipate the normal revolving-door-memberships that larger churches experience. But this was different: among the twelve families moving on were a couple of leaders in our church; a family I had walked with during a major crisis; two good friends who had been in our fellowship more than fifteen years; and a family who had excitedly joined our membership just three months earlier.

I had no clue that any of them were even considering making a change. So being the spiritually mature pastor I am, I threw a handful of self-pity party confetti in the air as I curmudgeonly signed their transfer letters, feeling more personal rejection than prayerful regard for these brothers and sisters.

BROKEN PEOPLE

The last appointment on my Thursday schedule before driving to the Art House left me numb and sick. John's story (a disguised identity) of childhood abuse and trauma rivals any I've ever heard in sheer evil. My new friend of six months grew up in a home in which he was beaten and berated consistently by his father, sexually molested by his older sister, and passively ignored by his nearly psychotic mother. This was his life, until the day he was tossed (set free?) from his home at the age of eighteen.

Understandably, John has been plagued with clinical depression for most of his fifty-plus years of life, and yet he is one of those 5 percent or so in our population who are labeled antidepressant resistant. This means he experiences no relief from the medications that often prove helpful to the other 95 percent of people who suffer with many of the cruel symptoms of depression.

On top of that, John rarely sleeps more than three hours a night. Why? Because his father used to say, over and over, "You can't trust anyone, so keep looking over your back. One night, somebody just might come in here [into his bedroom!] and take you out. So be careful." What kind of evil fills a father to so abuse his child?

Waiting for the film to begin, I could hear John's questions echoing, "Scotty, where was God when I was a little boy? If he knows all things, why did he knowingly put me into that family? Why didn't God rescue me then? Why won't he help me now?" I usually have answers, or at least words, for everything . . . but all I could do was listen and weep with my friend.

Broken Health

My wife, Darlene, was beaming with excitement. "Honey, I just served coffee to Mel Gibson, and he's so nice and he's not much taller than me!" But an all-too-familiar grimace quickly replaced her beautiful smile as she gingerly lowered herself into her chair.

For the last eighteen of our thirty-three years of marriage, I've watched my brave wife suffer with chronic and sometimes incapacitating pain.

The unfriendly conspiracy of a bulging disk, arthritis, and osteoporosis cause my fifty-three-year-old wife to feel like she's living in an eighty-year-old body. *How much is enough, Lord?* I thought to myself, wondering if she would even be able to sit long enough to see *The Passion*. Thankfully, a well-timed voice from the kitchen diverted my current train of thought. "OK, you guys, last call. Anybody need one more cup of coffee or another goodie? The film starts in five minutes."

A Mother's Flashback

The house lights dimmed, and the screen lit up. In anticipation of the post-film interaction with Mel Gibson, I adjusted my sometimes-film-critic, always-theologian hat. But it proved to be the wrong hat. I wasn't there to critique a movie but to experience The Story.

There's no way I could have anticipated the intensity and impact of those two hours. As one scene bled into another (quite literally), I felt myself becoming more and more emotionally connected with the humanity of Jesus, and with my own humanity as reflected in the confusion, distress, and weakness of the disciples.

As the film came to a merciful conclusion, we sat there stunned, dismantled, in awe—all forty of us trying to assimilate what we had just experienced. Like standing open-mouthed under Niagara Falls, it was impossible to drink in the undiluted rawness and hidden beauty of the last hours of Jesus' life. One brief scene, however, impacted us more than any other.

As Jesus painstakingly made His way to Calvary, we are invited to experience His grueling journey through the eyes and heart of His mother. Working her way through the pressing crowd, Mary edged closer and closer to her firstborn. She hoped for any chance to come alongside Jesus in His cruel aloneness, and positioned herself in a familiar alley. As the crucifixion entourage drew near to where Mary was standing, Jesus stumbled, falling down under the weight of the cross in the middle of a Jerusalem street.

Drawing from the vault of a mother's memory bank, the film flashes back to a much earlier time in Jesus' life. We see Jesus falling down as a little boy at play, on the same spot where He now lies as a grown man. The film succeeds in ripping our hearts with Mary's cruel impasse.

In both vignettes, she moved quickly to aid her son, instinctively doing what any loving mother would do. Lifting up her three- or four-year-old child, Mary held Jesus close to her heart, comforting Him with the incomparable balm of a mother's kisses. But now, three decades later, it would not be Mary, but others who would lift Jesus up—not to cuddle Him, but to crucify Him—not to ease His pain, but to increase it.

Exhausted, beaten, and wearing a crown of thorns intended to mock the very notion of His claim to *any* throne—Jesus gazed into His mother's distraught eyes, and, with the confidence of an unrivaled sovereign, He heralded new life for the entire universe in the ugly face of imminent death: *"Behold, woman, I make all things new!"*

I was caught *completely* off guard by this moment in the film. The contrast between the telling signs of defeat and the promise of cosmic renewal was stunning! *"Behold, woman, I make all things new!"* On one hand, Jesus' words came like a shocking bucket of cold water thrown into my face, because I had no way of anticipating this exchange between Jesus and Mary. On the other hand, it felt like a healing scalpel had been thrust into my heart. *"Behold, woman, I make all things new!"*

Though this promise thunders from heaven at a later time in Jesus' ministry (Revelation 21:5), the scriptwriters were theologically right to import it into this particular moment, whether they realized it or not. The cosmic implications of Jesus' imminent death and resurrection were captured in just a few frames of film and a few seconds of dialogue. *"Behold, woman, I make all things new!"*

A Son's Flash-Forward

This is why we call it *Good* Friday! As Jesus submitted to the Passion of that day, He knew the power of Resurrection Monday was coming . . . and He knew that the power of Resurrection Monday would lead, ultimately, to the glory of a completely renewed creation! The film shows us the first Easter as it unfolds, not just before our eyes, but through the eyes of Jesus. Easter must not be domesticated!

> Easter is the most thunderous moment in the whole year. Easter is such a huge event that even in the churches we can't cope with it, and we've scaled it down to fit our little minds. The world turns it into fluffy rabbits and chocolate eggs . . . We in the Church have (superficially) made Easter the source of our present (private) spiritual life: Jesus is alive today, so I can have a personal relationship with him. That's true; it's wonderful; but it is certainly not the full truth of Easter. . . .
>
> Easter isn't just about you and me and our present spiritual experience or our hope beyond the grave. Easter is the

beginning of God's new world. The idea of a "New Age," so popular just now, is a feeble pagan parody of the reality, which is this: that when Jesus burst out of the spiced tomb on the first Easter Day, the history of the cosmos changed its course. That's when the real New Age began. . . . Easter is the victory of the Creator over all evil. . . . It is the victory of the God of love over all tyranny. . . . It declares that, after all, God is God, and that his kingdom shall come and his will be done on earth as it is in heaven. Easter speaks of a world reborn.[1]

"Behold, I am making all things new!" Condemned as a criminal and dressed like a pauper, Mary's son, lying in the street under the weight of the cross, *is* a great *king*—a King like no other! *Humble enough* to die in the place of His faithless, rebellious subjects. *Powerful enough* to defeat death, crush the lord of darkness, and rise from His grave. *Loving enough* to give His people the life they do not deserve—eternal life—and the calling they cannot imagine: to be His cherished Bride forever. Jesus, the only King capable of creating a new world out of this broken one. *"Behold, I am making all things new!"*

I've ransacked emotional and theological thesauri looking for the right words to describe what I felt sitting in my Art House chair, but none seem adequate. There was a needed collision between Jesus' bold claim of restoration and the trainload of broken images weighing me down. I thought about my eighty-five-year-old dad, Darlene's pain, John's abuse, the cries of Africa, my own self-absorbed, petty heart . . . *"Behold, I am making all things new!"*

A world held emotionally hostage by the threat of terrorism. Friends divorcing. Genocide in Sudan. Church splits and loveless Christians. Staggering economic crises in third- and fourth-world countries. Escalating numbers of teenage suicides. Abortion on demand. Pornography on everything. Broken relationships. Cancer, cancer, and more cancer. Addictions galore. And now, as this book goes to press, the unconscionable and incalculable destruction of the South Asian tsunami. These things too, Jesus? *"Behold, I am making all things new!"*

BUT WHAT DOES IT MEAN?

I left the Art House that afternoon with significant hope and an insatiable hunger to explore Jesus' promise to make all things new. I didn't begin my study as a pastor looking for good sermon material, but as a broken man longing to understand and experience a greater measure of the restoration Jesus has secured by His death and resurrection. I began by making a list of questions generated by this one verse. I started with these:

"Behold . . ."

What do you want me to see, Jesus? What do I not see that I must see? Where do you want me to fix my gaze? What have I never seen about heaven that you now insist I behold?

"I am making all things new . . ."

What are you making new, Jesus? What is included in the "all things"? What does "brokenness" mean? What do you mean by

10

"new"? Jesus, *what on earth are you doing* today? How are you *presently* renewing the old and broken things? What are the evidences of this restoration, and how do you restore broken things? How much restoration can we expect in this life?

SEEING WHAT JOHN SAW TO LIVE AS JOHN LIVED

These questions propelled me to study and meditate upon the most complete picture God has given us of the "finished product"—the renewed world Jesus has committed to create out of this broken one. God entrusted the apostle John with a vision of this new-creation world to benefit the church of *every* generation. It's recorded for us in the last two chapters of Revelation.

It is in *this* context we hear the triumphant cry shouted from the throne in heaven, "*Behold, I am making all things new!*" (21:5). We must immerse ourselves in this part of God's Word if we are to understand Jesus' great promise of restoration.

But Revelation 21 and 22 are not just the last two chapters of the last book in the New Testament. They also own the distinction of being the last two chapters in the Bible taken as a *whole*—the fitting conclusion to God's one big Story, which begins in Genesis and continues to unfold through each of the sixty-six books of the Bible. *All* of the Scriptures anticipate and point toward the day when the magnificent universe and perfect society described in these two chapters will be finally and fully manifest.

To understand God's purposes, we need to return to the biblical story. One of the most important aspects of this story

11

relates to God's work relative to the presence of sin in the world. The biblical story has four unique chapters: Genesis 1–2 and Revelation 21–22. These chapters are unique in that no sin is present in the places and events described. Genesis 1–2 gives us a picture of God's creation design, what the world was like before sin entered the scene.

Revelation 21–22 gives us a picture of God's future intent, what the world will be like once redemption has been fully completed with the consummation of the judgment of sin and the evil one. These four chapters serve as bookends to the rest of the biblical story. The rest of the story is about the redemptive work of God in a sinful and fallen world. The story of re-creation relates the redemptive work of God to creation design by showing how He is restoring to *right relationship* that which was broken."[2]

It's *impossible* to appreciate the significance of the life, death, and resurrection of Jesus apart from "beholding" the vision of the new heaven and new earth that John records for us in Revelation 21–22. God is praised as we move from *polite amusement* to *impassioned astonishment* over the new-creation world of the future.

He began orienting His children toward this new world long before the apostle John received his vision. It was first through the prophet Isaiah that God promised, "Behold, I will create new heavens and a new earth. The former things will not be remembered. . . . But be glad and rejoice forever in what I will create" (Isaiah 65:17–18 NIV).

Amazing! God commands us to rejoice in what He has committed to create in the future. No other god *commands joy*, because no other god *compels joy*, except the one, true living God! He wants us to be *thoroughly* convinced of our future and familiar with the new world he is creating so that we live as its glad faithful citizens today!

But if Isaiah was privileged to hear the Architect dream out loud about His magnificent plans for a new development, then the apostle Paul owned a hardhat with his name on it, smelled the diesel exhaust of bulldozers, and walked the construction site. When Paul thought about God's new-creation world, he used strong emotional images that promise the emergence of life through great pain and present struggle. Paul's metaphor of choice in describing the new-creation world was a long, hard pregnancy with no chance of still-birth. The labor and delivery pains of childbirth will recede with the arrival of the promised new-creation world and new-creation family. Talk about multiple births!

> For the creation waits with eager longing for the revealing of the sons of God. For the creation was subjected to futility, not willingly, but because of him who subjected it, in hope that the creation itself will be set free from its bondage to decay and obtain the freedom of the glory of the children of God. For we know that the whole creation has been groaning together in the pains of childbirth until now (Romans 8:19–22).

Our calling is not just to see what John saw, but to live as John lived—faithfully loving and serving Jesus until the day all things are made perfectly and eternally new. Indeed, what could happen if our hearts get filled with a vision of the new world Jesus is creating?

2 THE IMPORTANCE OF STORY

"If you want people to hear the truth, tell them.
If you want people to know the truth, tell them a story."
— EUDORA WELTY

"A good story is the truth writ large."
— J. R. R. TOLKIEN

"All around God's story is coming alive,
and in this moment if we listen
We can hear Him calling,
Captivating, fascinating, all-consuming,
Never concluding . . . one and only . . . ever unfolding
. . . Story of stories"
— SCC, "Big Story"

(STEVEN):

I remember when me and Jack Martin . . ." Those seven words were music to my ears and the prelude to some of my favorite moments with my dad. Holding forth in the stern of our little fishing boat, Dad introduced me to the world of story, fueling my imagination and igniting my passion to experience life as a Technicolor expedition and escapade the way *he* did. My dad never

15

read me a Hardy Boys story . . . because he *was* a Hardy Boy, and he made me want to become one too.

"Steven, one time, (me and Jack) snuck into an abandoned house that was for sale. I wish you could have seen it, son! We found a pair of old cowboy boots in a closet and strategically placed them behind the living room curtains with the scuffed toes sticking out underneath about three inches, facing toward the center of the room. Next, we took a kitchen broom and leaned it *perfectly*, creating a suspicious bulge in the curtain about five feet above the boots, making it look like someone was hiding behind it."

How fitting that dad's best storytelling was showcased on our fishing trips, for fishermen love to add inches and pounds to "the big one that got away," and embellish the accounts of the fish that actually make it into the boat. Though I never knew when dad crossed the line from exactitude to exaggeration, it didn't really matter. He wasn't lying; he was coming alive, and I fed off his energy.

"When we got everything set up just like we wanted it, (me and Jack) went outside and found a good place to hide in the bushes, anxious to see who would be the first to have the 'bejeebies' scared out of them. Just as we settled down into our hideout, a realtor drove up with an elderly couple. As he unlocked the front door of the house, our palms got sweaty and hearts started racing like crazy.

"They were only in the house a few minutes when, all of a sudden, the glass door flew open and nearly came off its hinges. And like a triple jumper at the Olympics, that granny bounded out of the house like she was fifty years younger . . . yelling, running, and carrying on. I'm tellin' ya, we nearly wet our pants!"

Dad wasn't retelling this story; he was reliving it. And like the little boy in one of my favorite TV commercials—who after watching a mesmerizing summer sunset with his dad, exclaims, "Do it again, Daddy, do it again!"—I could have listened to my dad tell that same story again *right then*, and it would have been just as entertaining as the first time. But it was more than entertaining, enthralling, and empowering. It made me want to look for a "For Sale" sign in front of an abandoned house in *our* neighborhood, so I could go and do the same thing.

Indeed, Dad's storytelling marked me. He gave me a love for the power of story and a hunger to experience adventuresome stories of my own. No doubt, this is the reason why, as a believer, I'm more often impacted by a powerful biography than by a well-reasoned teaching, and it's why so many of my songs are story-based.

The written epistles of God's Word come alive to me best through the living epistles of His family—God's sons and daughters reliving their stories of adventures in His kingdom, showing what can happen when the love and grace of Jesus deeply penetrate and liberate the lives of ordinary people like you and me. Printed propositions in the Bible are meant to be brought to life through passionate people—that's the heart of the gospel. It's the incarnation of Jesus, who was the "Word made flesh" for us.

The more I learn about and engage with *God's* Story, the more one of my older songs has taken on new meaning and a radical redefinition. In *The Great Adventure*, I used the Wild West imagery of saddling and mounting up on our horses, inviting all of us to "gitty-up" and raise a cloud of dust as we head into the adventures of life in the kingdom of God.

But several years, tears, and stories later—after trips into the squalor of Africa, the stark reality of death row, the jungles of Ecuador, the vastness of China, and a three-daughter journey into the world of adoption—I realize what I *used* to consider great adventure simply required mounting painted, carousel ponies you can find at the state fair or any traveling carnival. What we *really* need—for the Story and the adventures into which Jesus has called us—is the combination of a pack mule for strength, a camel for perseverance, and a quarter horse for speed. Though we may not find such an animal, God has promised that we'll have everything we need for the journey.

The Story from Which All Stories Flow

Our book begins with a story about *story*, as a prelude to telling *the* Story of *all* stories! That's not a riddle, but an important orientation. The twenty-first century has dawned as an era of *story*. There are more books, seminars, and educators emphasizing the importance and power of *story* than at any time in the history of American culture. We are becoming a "narrative nation," as a friend recently described—a people weary of cliché, cynical about dogma, and starving for the authenticity of personal story. This hunger for *story* is nowhere more evident than within the contemporary church.

Instead of testimonies, we are learning to *share our stories*. Instead of the old-school, three-point-sermon, pastors are developing *narrative preaching* styles. Instead of getting together with friends for a chat or just to hang out, we meet at Starbucks to *update our stories*. In the age-old continuum of "show and tell," our culture seems to be crying for a lot more *showing* (inviting) and a lot less *telling* (indicting).

Is *story* one more fad of a pop culture insatiably committed to relevance? Hardly, for we carry the structure and rhythm of story in our DNA. As John Eldredge says, "Life does not come to us as a math problem, but scene by scene. . . . Life unfolds like a drama. Sometimes it seems like a tragedy. Sometimes like a comedy. Most of it feels like a soap opera. Whatever happens, it's a story through and through."[1]

We love stories, and we live by stories because we cannot do otherwise. Just as cocoa beans were predestined to become dark chocolate, and Paul McCartney for writing great music, so *we* were designed for the joy of *story*. God reveals himself in the Bible as a *personal* God who calls us into the dynamics of relationship, not into the dogmatics of religion. To be made in God's image is to be created with an instinct and penchant for story—*God's* Story, or, as C. S. Lewis calls it, "the Great Story which goes on forever in which every chapter is better than the one before."

My *Story* Story

(Scotty:)

For the most part, I now welcome this emphasis on *story*, but only after crossing over the half-century mark in life. I take some consolation in realizing that Frodo and Sam were also fifty when they connected with "storied living"—leaving the predictable routines of the Shire for the wild adventures of *The Lord of the Rings*. And wasn't Moses eighty when he moved from the backside of a desert more fully into God's Story? What's taken me so long to connect with the *story* dimensions of Christian spirituality?

In elementary school, I loved it when one of my teachers would launch into a "story moment"—either intentionally, or through our diversionary tactics as crafty students. Tales of *any* kind held far more sway than abstract numbers, meaningless dates, and rules of grammar. Stories delayed, at least briefly, the inevitable measuring rod of quizzes and exams. I knew a test was lurking just around the corner of each new dump-truck load of information. The floating anxiety of being celebrated or chided, based on my ability to regurgitate information on exams, was ever present.

Henri Nouwen understood how I felt: "The world in which I have grown up is a world so full of grades, scores, and statistics that, consciously or unconsciously, I always try to take my measure against all the others. Much sadness and gladness in my life flows directly from my comparing, and most, if not all, of this comparing is useless and a terrible waste of time and energy."[2]

Especially as children, we intuitively know (or desperately hope) we've been made for more than living from report card to report card. And stories have a way of tapping into something more eternal and holy than memorizing material and scorecard living. As a child, these stories watered my imagination garden, which was left barren by too much television, too little reading, and too little conversation. They were the bell on the ice-cream truck occasionally driving through the neighborhood of my bland dream world. I wasn't read to at home, and neither did I read to myself, probably because I couldn't sit still very long, except in front of the TV.

Unfortunately, television essentially defined the boundaries of my dreams and imagination, as it did for so many others. In a world exploding with colors, textures, and dimensions, I couldn't see much beyond the universe that the *Little Rascals* and the *Three Stooges* were showing me.

The transition from the fifth grade into the sixth was a traumatic one, as I went from having teachers *read* me stories to having to *write my own*—which I hated. That was also the year I was introduced to book reports, to which I developed an immediate allergy. Being a nonreader, I would skim a few chapters and offer a general impression of the book. Or many times, I would create a fictitious book title and author, and turn in a complete lie. That's how averse I was to reading.

But the most difficult transition that the sixth grade brought started seven weeks into the school year on the afternoon I got word my mother had been killed in a car wreck. My already stunted ability to dream, imagine, and feel was frozen and buried with Mom, where it stayed entombed for nearly forty years. I became Peter Pan without a Neverland, He Beaver without a Narnia, and Winnie the Pooh without a Corner. Story moments were replaced with moment-by-moment attempts to stay numb and survive an awkward and lonely trek into adolescence.

FROM HERE TO MODERNITY

Seven years later, in 1968, as a senior in high school, I became a follower of Jesus through the persistent prodding of a friend. I began my infancy in Christ in the cultural nursery of "modernity"—the worldview shaped by the values of Enlightenment and the Industrial Revolution that had prevailed in the West since the eighteenth century.

A worldview functions like a set of corrective lenses; it affects how we perceive and experience the individual things we encounter in the world. It also acts like a picture frame, providing a frame of reference by which the individual things of life are seen in their relationship to one another.

Though a biblical worldview is beginning to develop, we don't easily jettison one worldview for another. We tend to wear multiple lenses, and we get scratches and grime on our lenses, for we are broken and inconsistent people. Only in the past several years have I come to see how modernity impacted me spiritually. Tom Wright identified three core characteristics of modern man as the "modernist trinity."

First, modern man is the self-sufficient, competent individual—the master of his fate, the captain of his soul. He believes he can accomplish *anything* he sets his mind to do. *Second*, modern man has a certainty about the world and his objective knowledge of it. Empirical verification and rational prowess have replaced the superstitions and religious "hocus-pocus" of the pre-scientific medieval world. *Third*, and perhaps most telling of all, modern man has created and embraced a new mythology—the myth of progress. Shedding the archaic rubrics of fear and fantasies, modern man sees himself as having attained "enlightenment." Evolution *will* win. Modern man's mantra? "It's getting better all the time."

This new "trinity" established an invisible but impenetrable line between "objective facts" and "subjective values"—in essence, separating heaven and earth, and God and man. *Real* truth began to be confirmed in the laboratories of science and the academy of rationality. Religious thought and experience were relegated to an altogether different sphere of life, never to intrude into the *real* world. The Bible was demythologized and became inspirational but not instructive—to be used in the background of culture as theological elevator music or in the private lives of those "who need that sort of thing." The consequences of this worldview soon became evident. Traditional ethics became situational, and traditional religion became recreational.

JUST GIVE ME THE FACTS

My first collision with the undiluted, in-your-face assumptions of modernity occurred during my freshman year at the University of North Carolina. After being convinced God was leading me into vocational ministry, I changed my major from pharmacy to religion during my first semester.

Having ten times more zeal than knowledge, it was difficult to have most of my professors in the religion department cavalierly dismiss the Scriptures as *myths* and *religious stories* that, as one professor said, are "no more helpful than Aesop's fables, and, in some ways, more dangerous [if taken seriously] than 'Mao's little red book.'"

Thus, *story* became synonymous with a low view of the Bible's inspiration and a high disdain for the truth claims of conservative Christianity. I developed a knee-jerk reaction whenever anyone talked about the Bible, God, or Jesus in terms of *story.* Webster's Dictionary helped confirm my suspicion by associating *story* with words like *tale, yarn, legend, fairy tale, anecdote, rumor, hearsay, buzz, untruth, fib,* and *falsehood.*

Gasoline was poured on this already steadily burning, anti-story flame when one of my instructors at Westminster Seminary recounted the day he defended his master's thesis before esteemed theologian Dr. Paul Tillich. In this snapshot, notice the distinction made between rationality and religious inspiration. The closing moments of the spirited oral exam went like this:

"Well, Bob, one final question. If you'd been present with a camera on the day of Jesus' resurrection and had taken His picture outside of the tomb, would anything have shown up on the developed film?" "Yes, Dr. Tillich, Jesus would have been clearly identifiable in that photograph."

At that point in the spirited interchange, my instructor described watching his master's thesis sail through the air across the room, as Dr. Tillich lamented, "Then I have failed you! What matters is the hope born from the *story* and symbol of resurrection, not the proof of an empty tomb! Dead men don't rise from the grave, but living men need to hope!"

My anger piqued as I sat there listening to this account, and for good reason. Call me old-fashioned, but the *story* or *fable* of Jesus' resurrection doesn't seem to offer quite as much hope as the assurance of His *actual* resurrection. The apostle Paul called faith *futile*, sins *unforgiven*, dead Christians *lost,* and living Christians most *pitiable* if Jesus was not raised from the dead (1 Corinthians 15:17–19).

And yet my holding onto the *fact* of the Resurrection often didn't function very differently from Paul Tillich's holding onto the *idea* of the Resurrection. Living from your head is living from your head, no matter how you dress it up. If our lives don't demonstrate the power of Jesus' resurrection, then our words are simply hot air, even if our arguments are air-tight.

STRAIGHTJACKETS ON OUR HEARTS

I became preoccupied with apologetics (the defense of the faith) and arguing for truthfulness of Christianity. I spent more time building a case for the authority of the Bible than I did in reading the contents of the Bible. Coming to Christ did not instantaneously make this nonreader a reader, but it did inspire me to acquire knowledge, or at least information.

To further bolster my defensive arsenal, I became increasingly attracted to the study of systematic theology and the seemingly irrefutable logic of reformed theology. Satisfying answers and confidence in "being right" gave me a sense of control and security.

As I reflect on the first several years of life as a believer, I truly lament this part of my story. I became a theological talking head, more passionately invested in knowing the propositions of the faith than knowing the Person at the center of the faith: Jesus. While I busied myself with the credibility of the Bible, I missed the beauty of its story.

Yet even a casual reading of the New Testament reveals Jesus' choice of story, especially parables, as His primary vehicle for teaching. Jesus came into the world on a bridal mission, not merely on a lecture tour. To be a follower of Jesus is to be called into the love story from which all love stories derive their meaning.

God has used a steady stream of circumstances and people to address this corruption of His Story. I'll meet one of these people for the first time in heaven, but while writing this book I feel like I have gotten to know him as a friend: C. S. Lewis, the great English writer and Oxford scholar. I leaned heavily on "Jack's" intellectual prowess in the late-'60s as a way of convincing myself I wasn't committing cognitive hari-kari to be a follower of Jesus. And yet little did I realize, until this year, just how much we have in common (not on a gift level, mind you!). His story has helped me understand my own.

As a nine-year-old child, Lewis also experienced the tragic death of his mother. And, like me, it marked him as no other single event before coming to faith in Jesus. This wound, combined with his education in the rigors of logic and the rigidity of his childhood spiritual influences, "conspired to put his heart in a straightjacket." How I relate to that! Only in his late forties was Lewis able to break free into the world of feeling and story. He didn't leave his brilliant mind behind, but simply entered the world of imagination and emotion that God has given each of us.

Author Madeleine L'Engle described the joy of watching God's grace bring healing and freedom to Lewis's heart—a process revealed sequentially as each of his writings were published. The first book she read by Lewis was *The Problem of Pain*, and it elicited, in her words:

> outrage . . . [for] he showed a total lack of sensitivity toward the pain of animals. . . . That pain is part of the pain of the world; if it doesn't matter then nothing matters. I put Lewis aside. . . . Then someone gave me *Out of the Silent Planet*. No longer was I being preached at, coldly and unlovingly (as I then felt), but I was given story. Here was a world where I too could live; characters with whom I could identify. . . .
>
> I was growing and changing. So was he. How strange it is that we grow more in doing the things we think we cannot do than in the things we think are possible or permissible!

Lewis' theology lost its academic quality after he married Joy Davidman, and became infused with love. We have a tendency today to want people to be consistent; we change; we dwindle or we grow, and Lewis grew. His theology became more human as he grew through his surprises with joy and his battle with pain.[3]

AN EMERGING STORY

It's been thirty-seven years since I responded to the offer of eternal life in Jesus—long enough to have watched the positivism of modernity get challenged, and largely replaced with the suspicion, cynicism, and "deconstructionism" of *postmodernism*. If modernity said, "The spiritual emperor doesn't have any clothes on," then postmodernity is saying, "*Nobody* has any clothes on in the public square."

Everybody and everything is up for deconstructionist grabs. The line between test-tube facts and spiritual experience, and between belief and unbelief has moved. In fact, *all* lines have been erased. What features of the postmodern worldview stand out?

Instead of objective facts—hard-edged things, like lumps of coal or steel girders—we have impressions, attitudes and feelings. . . . Facts are not important; spin is everything. . . . Reality is no longer divided, as by modernity, into facts and values, or truths of reason and truths of science. It is whatever you make of it. You invent it as you go along. Choose your value and the story will follow. . . . "We have nothing else other than the meaning we create." . . .

One of postmodernity's best-known features is the so-called "death of the metanarrative." "Metanarratives" are the overarching stories which give meaning to all the smaller stories of our normal existence. . . . Postmodernity has claimed that all such larger stories are destructive and enslaving, and must be rejected. . . . All we are left with, then, is a plurality of stories—your story, my story. . . . Metanarratives are deemed to be oppressive; freedom consists in telling and living by our own mini-stories, and our own local stories. . . . [But] nobody functions according to only one story. We are each a mass of floating impulses and impressions, changing all the time, reconstructing ourselves as we go along according to the stimuli we receive, the spin that comes our way.[4]

This explains why the category of *story* is so important in the emerging postmodern world. Stories describe without prescribing. They reveal without regulating and communicate without controlling. It has been the postmodernist's loud protestation against all "metanarratives" (overarching "big stories" that give meaning and coherence to the little stories of life) that has forced me to see just how central the construct of story is to all of life.

A Grander Narrative

As much as I tried to suppress it, *story* came onto the scene in my life, front and center, and with a vengeance! Schooled and skilled in reactionary thinking and living, I began to ponder postmodernity's adamant rejection of the Bible as one more metanarrative. The principal reason "big stories" are suspect is the assumption that *all* of them are exploitive power plays that enslave and oppress those under their sway, from communism to capitalism to consumerism to Christianity, etc.

On one hand, guilty as charged! The postmodernist is *right* to classify the Bible as a metanarrative, for the Scriptures *do* tell a story that connects and claims to bring meaning to all the smaller stories of life—and, for that matter, to *all* of history. But do we think it's a mere coincidence that *two-thirds* of the Bible has been written in the style, rhythm, and structure of *story*? Michael Green writes:

> The Bible is a story, and it contains within its grand metanarrative many stories. . . . But essentially it is one story, the story of God's romance with the world—God's unquenchable and gratuitous love for humankind. As a story it has a beginning, middle, and an end. It is going somewhere. But it is also taking us with it. Because the biblical story is the grand story of who we are, who the God we are dealing with is, and what it all means—it is a story that enfolds our own stories in a grander narrative.[5]

That "grander narrative" is a grand story indeed, for the Bible doesn't encourage the abuse of power or the oppression of the masses. Just the opposite: God's Story is "taking us with it" into Jesus' commitment to *demolish* all systemic evil, injustice, and oppression. God's Story condemns *all* forms of corruption and abuse, and zealously advocates for the marginalized and neglected members of society, such as the poor, widows, and orphans. It's *this* part of God's Story which has propelled Steven Curtis's family into the redemptively messy and inconvenient lifestyle of adoption.

Indeed, story must not become for us just another metaphor for personal fulfillment. Anne Lamott writes, "A human life is like a single letter of the alphabet. It can be meaningless. Or it can be a part of a great meaning."[6] God delights to make words, sentences, and paragraphs of grace through the broken and rebellious letters written into the "grander narrative."

CHARACTERS AND CARRIERS

As followers of Jesus, we've been placed not just in a *big* story, but also in a much *better* story than our lives demonstrate. We've got a long history of hypocrisy and inconsistency, which the Bible itself chronicles. God is telling an authentic, non-spin story of selfish, broken people, who are in the process of being made new by Jesus. That's why *Jesus* has the lead role in God's Story. But He's not the only character.

He's making *us* characters too. We are *carriers* of God's Story—targets for hope who'll serve as agents of hope, and candidates of mercy who'll live as conduits of mercy. Jesus is bringing restoration to broken individuals as a means of bringing healing to *other* individuals, families, communities, and, ultimately, to the whole universe.

The Bible tells a story of *personal*, not *privatized* blessing. God's Story is not a metaphor for self-actualization or a vehicle of personal validation. It's to be the means by which narcissists become servant neighbors, materialists become material witnesses to the outrageous generosity of Jesus, and the conceited develop an astonishing concern for the least and the lost in society.

If Steven and I are going to be redundant about any one theme in our book it is this: we are made to live in God's Story . . . for God's glory . . . with God's joy. It's only within *God's* Story that *our* stories find their true meaning and destiny. *This* is the story that we have in common with God's people of *every* generation.

Think about it: though we spend much of life relegating God to bit parts in our little autobiographies of self-fulfillment, God generously "enfolds" us into His cosmic Story of transforming love! Could any of us possibly want or hope for more out of life?

We are called into a story that *enfolds our own stories in a grander narrative*—a story that is *going somewhere*, a story that is *taking us with it*. There really is a Great Story that goes on forever, in which each chapter gets better than the one before. We dwindle or we grow. Which will you choose?

3 ENGAGING WITH GOD'S STORY OF RESTORATION

"Then I saw a new heaven and a new earth, for the first heaven and the first earth had passed away, and the sea was no more."
—REVELATION 21:1

"I hear the rumors of another world,
like distant voices in the wind
They say there is a story being told
bigger than I can comprehend
And in the rumors I can hear an invitation calling"
— SCC, "Big Story"

(STEVEN):

I'd just finished a pregame devotional for the Los Angeles Dodgers, who were in Atlanta for a series with the Braves.

"Was Kevin Brown there?" Mary Beth asked the question with so much enthusiasm and hope, it was obvious she anticipated a straight-up, affirmative answer.

I paused before responding, because if eating depended on beating my wife in sports trivia, I'd die a hungry man. Mary Beth's understanding of the rules of the games is just as impressive (and scary) as her knowledge of the players.

"Let's see, well, ugh . . . Kevin *who*, sweetheart?" I meagerly responded, bracing myself for an impassioned reply.

"*Steven* . . . the Dodgers just signed Kevin Brown to one of the biggest contracts in the history of professional baseball. *What do you mean 'Kevin who?'*"

"Oh, *thaaat* Kevin. Yeah, I think he was there." Even over the phone, I could tell Mary Beth was rolling her eyes, and both of us knew my cluelessness about sporting greatness had just been exposed—once again.

If Mary Beth ever wanted to exchange places with me, it would probably be during the times I get to meet and share with many of our nation's most celebrated professional teams. In the past few years, I've been honored with a "baptism" into the world of professional sports . . . singing the national anthem at both an NBA game between the Phoenix Suns and San Antonio Spurs, and an NHL game, while Wayne Gretsky was still skating for the Los Angeles Kings. Scotty and I led a chapel service together for the then-Mike-Ditka-coached New Orleans Saints, who were in town for a game with our Titans. And I even had a quarterback for the Pittsburgh Steelers, Tommy Maddox, blow me away by crediting one of my songs, "Dive," for inspiring his incredible comeback a few years ago. A friendship that I continue to cherish was born out of that encounter.

I will never better Mary Beth when it comes to recognizing new offensive formations, knowing the rules of cross-checking, and keeping up with the breaking news about player trades and contract negotiations. Nevertheless, the privilege of attending all of these amazing sporting events and watching the top athletes in the world perform before tens of thousands of fans in the finest arenas in our country has left me with one *huge* impression: there are *way* too many of us sitting in the stands—wearing our team's jersey, munching away on our nachos and pizza—who offer criticism about games we don't really understand, and for coaches and players with whom we share *no* relationship. When our team wins, we take credit for victories in which we played *no part* whatsoever. I've seen this pattern in professional football, baseball, basketball, and hockey. Unfortunately, this same trend—of being ill-informed, armchair quarterbacks who seldom break a sweat—seems to apply to our spiritual life as a nation just as much as it does to our sporting life.

Knowing and Engaging

But God is calling each of us *to know* and *to engage* with His magnificent story of cosmic restoration through Jesus. This means we are to learn *the content* and *contours* of God's Story, *and* we are to become both *characters in* and *carriers of* His Big Story. We can't afford to be ignorant of the game, nor is there any place for armchair quarterbacking. We're *all* called to get out of the stands and into the action—together.

The apostle John models both of these elements for us as the author of the Book of Revelation. He shows us that *understanding* and *experience* come together most powerfully at the intersection of the stories in which we participate. We are to follow John's example. As we begin our study of John's vision of the "all-things-new world" Jesus is creating (Revelation 21:1–22:5), a brief introduction to the context and larger story being told in Revelation would be helpful.

THE WONDER OF IT ALL

Like Moses, the apostle John began one of the most significant chapters in his journey of faith as a member of the eighty-year-old club. Roman persecution was mounting against the followers of Jesus in the last quarter of the first century, forcing the aging apostle into exile on a rocky isle called Patmos. Thirty-seven miles of Aegean Sea separated John from the lambs under his pastoral care, but *nothing* separated him from the presence of the Good Shepherd. The opening verse of Revelation sets the focus and tone of the whole letter.

"The revelation of Jesus Christ, which God gave him to show his servants what must soon take place" (1:1 NIV). Jesus is presented as the source and substance of Revelation. This is a letter *from* Jesus and *about* Jesus. John, the scribe, is simply called to unveil Christ's glory and grace to the seven churches of Asia Minor, all placed within a ninety-mile radius of one another in the contemporary region of Turkey.

As the courier read John's circular letter to each church, they would be reminded that Christians, more so than anything else, are called to "make much of Jesus"—to understand and experience Jesus as the beginning, middle, and end of God's whole Story.

Thus, great blessing is promised to "the one who reads the words of this prophecy" and to those who "hear it and take to heart what is written in it" (v. 3 NIV). Why? Because it comes to us from the One who can be trusted implicitly—Jesus, "the faithful witness" (v. 5 NIV).

Jesus can be trusted by those experiencing persecution and those facing martyrdom, for He is "the firstborn from the dead" (v. 5 NIV).

His resurrection is the guarantee of our future resurrection. Jesus can be trusted by those living in a world of pervasive evil and tyrannical rulers, for He is "the ruler of kings on earth" (v. 5 NIV). Jesus can be trusted by the shamed, broken, and marginalized because He "loves us and has freed us from our sins by his blood, and has made us to be a kingdom and priests to serve his God and Father" (vv. 5-6 NIV).

And Jesus can be trusted by the fearful and anxious, for He speaks words of powerful hope to John and to all of us: "Do not be afraid. I am the First and the Last. I am the Living One; I was dead, and behold I am alive for ever and ever! And I hold the keys of death and Hades"—and nobody else does! (vv. 17–18 NIV).

Not only can Jesus be trusted, He is worthy to receive all worship, all "power and wealth and wisdom and might and honor and glory and blessing" (5:12) because He is "the Lion of the tribe of Judah, the Root of David" (5:5). He fulfilled God's promise of a great King and His commitment to establish an eternal kingdom of peace (Genesis 49:9–10; 2 Samuel 7:12–16; Isaiah 6:13; 11:1). Christ is the Lamb of God who "purchased men for God from every tribe and language and people and nation" (Revelation 5:9 NIV) by the shedding of His blood upon the Cross. He completed God's promise to redeem an every-nation-people for Himself (Genesis 12–17; Isaiah 52:13–53:12).

This triumphant affirmation of who Jesus is, and what He has done, saturates *every* vision, hymn, war, scene, conflict, and symbol contained in all twenty-two chapters of Revelation, culminating in John's exhilarating description of the new heaven and new earth (21:1–22:5).

Knee-Buckling, Face-Planting Wonder

Like a play-by-play announcer trying to contain himself as he describes the ending of the greatest Super Bowl ever played, John was overwrought with unspeakable joy. His knees buckled, and his face was planted in the soil in true worship (Revelation 19:10; 22:8). His dazzling and animated vision of the future of heaven was given to encourage the young church to remain faithful and fearless as they served their loving Bridegroom in every season of life. Though these believers had been taught that God would "bring to completion the good work he has begun" (Philippians 1:6, translation mine), surely a peek at just *how* good the "completed work" would be could keep them engaged with God's Story of restoration as they faced much temptation and opposition. Of this coming world, Graeme Goldsworthy writes:

> The new heaven and the new earth described by John in Revelation 21:1–22:5 is the resolution of all conflict, suffering, and meaninglessness in life. There can be no longer any deficiencies in the relationship between God, man, and the created order. The overlap of the ages ceases as this present world order in which we live is removed with all the evil that characterizes it. Through resurrection and glorification the believer is brought fully into the regeneration of all things. The new age alone becomes the reality of his existence. This is the realm in which the effects of Christ's life and death are perceived and experienced in all their fullness.[1]

Take a moment to read John's words with the childlike wonder with which he recorded them. Perhaps you'd like to have a pen and notebook close by to mark particular verses, or to write down a few impressions or questions as they come to you. Don't get mired down trying to understand every image. We'll explore most of the symbols in coming chapters. Here's the way John experienced as much of the new heaven and new earth as Jesus revealed to him:

> Then I saw a new heaven and a new earth, for the first heaven and the first earth had passed away, and the sea was no more. And I saw the holy city, new Jerusalem, coming down out of heaven from God, prepared as a bride adorned for her husband.
>
> And I heard a loud voice from the throne saying, "Behold, the dwelling place of God is with man. He will dwell with them, and they will be his people, and God himself will be with them as their God. He will wipe away every tear from their eyes, and death shall be no more, neither shall there be mourning nor crying nor pain anymore, for the former things have passed away." And he who was seated on the throne said, "Behold, I am making all things new." Also he said, "Write this down, for these words are trustworthy and true."
>
> And he said to me, "It is done! I am the Alpha and the Omega, the beginning and the end. To the thirsty I will give from the spring of the water of life without payment. The one who conquers will have this heritage, and I will be his God and he will be my son. But as for

the cowardly, the faithless, the detestable, as for murderers, the sexually immoral, sorcerers, idolaters, and all liars, their portion will be in the lake that burns with fire and sulfur, which is the second death."

Then came one of the seven angels who had the seven bowls full of the seven last plagues and spoke to me, saying, "Come, I will show you the Bride, the wife of the Lamb." And he carried me away in the Spirit to a great, high mountain, and showed me the holy city Jerusalem coming down out of heaven from God, having the glory of God, its radiance like a most rare jewel, like a jasper, clear as crystal. It had a great, high wall, with twelve gates, and at the gates twelve angels, and on the gates the names of the twelve tribes of the sons of Israel were inscribed—on the east three gates, on the north three gates, on the south three gates, and on the west three gates.

And the wall of the city had twelve foundations, and on them were the twelve names of the twelve apostles of the Lamb. And the one who spoke with me had a measuring rod of gold to measure the city and its gates and walls. The city lies foursquare; its length the same as its width. And he measured the city with his rod, 12,000 stadia. Its length and width and height are equal. He also measured its wall, 144 cubits by human measurement, which is also an angel's measurement. The wall was built of jasper, while the city was pure gold, clear as glass.

The foundations of the wall of the city were adorned with every kind of jewel. The first was jasper, the second sapphire, the third agate, the fourth emerald, the fifth onyx, the sixth carnelian, the seventh chrysolite, the eighth beryl, the ninth topaz, the tenth chrysoprase, the eleventh jacinth, the twelfth amethyst. And the twelve gates were twelve pearls, each of the gates made of a single pearl, and the street of the city was pure gold, transparent as glass.

And I saw no temple in the city, for its temple is the Lord God the Almighty and the Lamb. And the city has no need of sun or moon to shine on it, for the glory of God gives it light, and its lamp is the Lamb. By its light will the nations walk, and the kings of the earth will bring their glory into it, and its gates will never be shut by day—and there will be no night there. They will bring into it the glory and the honor of the nations. But nothing unclean will ever enter it, nor anyone who does what is detestable or false, but only those who are written in the Lamb's book of life.

Then the angel showed me the river of the water of life, bright as crystal, flowing from the throne of God and of the Lamb through the middle of the street of the city; also, on either side of the river, the tree of life with its twelve kinds of fruit, yielding its fruit each month. The leaves of the tree were for the healing of the nations. No longer will there be anything accursed, but the throne of God and of the Lamb will be in it, and his servants will worship him. They will see his face, and his name will be on their foreheads. And night will be no more. They will need no light of lamp or sun, for the Lord God will be their light, and they will reign forever and ever (Revelation 21:1–22:5).

THE RICHES OF ONE VERSE

Granted, there is a *whole lot* of rich material in this one passage to understand—much more than we can possibly hope to explain in this little book. But if you will take the time to become familiar with the main themes of this portion of God's Word, it can open the whole Bible to you. In fact, the first verse of this passage is truly remarkable. Before John shows us the *scenery* of the new world, he tells us the *story* of the new world.

In just one sentence of twenty-seven words, John summarizes the *entire* storyboard of the Bible, by presenting the four elements of its plot. "Then I saw a new heaven and a new earth, for the first heaven and the first earth had passed away, and the sea was no more" (21:1).

What are the four plot elements of the one Big Story that God is telling in the Bible?

CREATION > FALL > REDEMPTION > CONSUMMATION

In a moment, we'll see how each of these plot elements is revealed in John's twenty-seven-word sentence, and we'll explore them in detail. But before we do, consider how each of us processes God's ultimate Story with regard to these elements.

Don't Edit It . . . Engage It!

In a world of DVD technology, it's easy to become the producer and editor of our own movies. All we have to do is advance to the DVD scene menu, click the appropriate numbers for our scenes of choice, and record them onto a disc. Voilà! Instant movie mogul, instant gratification!

While there are certain benefits to this editorial freedom, consider the downside. Let's say you created an edited version of all of your DVD movies, only recording your favorite scenes. A friend borrows a few of these edited movies, not realizing that they've been altered.

His opinion of each movie, whether good or bad, will be entirely based on a *distortion of the scenes* because of a *corruption of its original plot*. The *intended* meaning of the *individual parts* of a story can only be discovered and experienced in the context of the *whole story*. And this is just as true for the Bible as it is for your favorite novel or movie. Too many of us have formed our opinion about the Bible based on a distortion of its individual stories through a corruption of its original plot. How does this play out?

Load your DVD player with "The DVD Bible." With clicker in hand, and a love for the "theme of redemption," go to the scene selection menu and click on some of your favorite stories of redemption from the Old and New Testaments: "The Return of the Prodigal Son," "The Love Story Between Ruth and Boaz," "The Apostle Paul and John Mark Are Reunited," "Joseph's Reconciliation with His Abusive Brothers," etc. Now record these scenes onto a disc without regard for their context in individual books of the Bible or the larger context of the whole Bible. Surely this would provide an accurate picture of the Bible's overall redemptive message, right?

Wrong. To start with, *Redemption* is not a *metaphorical theme,* but an *historical event* in the Bible. *Redemption* centers on the person and work of Jesus Christ. All "redemptive stories" in the Bible are meant to be understood and experienced in relationship to Jesus' life, death, and resurrection. That's why, for instance, Jesus shows up *everywhere* in the brief introduction to Revelation we looked at earlier. If the Bible does only one thing, that one thing is to *make much of Jesus.* Jesus is the main character in the one Big Story the Bible is telling.

Take George Bailey (Jimmy Stewart's character) out of *It's a Wonderful Life,* or Indiana Jones (Harrison Ford) out of *Indiana Jones and the Last Crusade,* or William Wallace (Mel Gibson) out of *Braveheart,* and what've you got? The same thing you'd get if you took Jesus (Jim Caviezel) out of *The Passion of the Christ* . . . a gutted and corrupted version of the whole story. But there's more.

RESTORATION HARDWARE

The word *Redemption,* by definition, means "a buying back" or "a buying of freedom." It evokes images of hostages or kidnapees being released. Technically, something is redeemed when it is rescued, retrieved by payment, and returned to an original state or condition. Therefore, redemption presupposes two important states: the *original condition,* before there was a need for redemption, and the *altered condition,* which created the need for redemption. In the Bible, the *original condition* is known as *Creation* and the *altered condition* is referred to as the *Fall.* Let's start putting this together.

For example: to understand what the Bible means by *Redemption*

44

of man, we must first of all discover what the Bible says about the *Creation* of man. *Creation* reveals the original *design and purpose* God gave to mankind. A restored antique table is only as valuable as how well the restoration accurately re-created what that table was like when brand new. This same principle applies to the *Redemption* of man. By examining our original state, we can establish a starting point on which we can evaluate the degree of redemption.

But we also need to discover man's condition resulting from the *Fall*. For unless we see the contrast between *Creation* and *Fall*, we cannot possibly understand what kind of *Redemption* will be required to redeem a man. There's a big difference between falling off a two-foot ladder and falling off a cliff into the Grand Canyon. The results call for two very different redemptions—one from embarrassment and one from death!

Fall is shorthand for "falling from glory and breaking," which describes the tragic, resulting condition when sin and death permeates every aspect of God's creation (Genesis 3). Remember this childhood rhyme?

> *Humpty Dumpty sat on a wall.*
> *Humpty Dumpty had a great fall.*
> *All of the king's horses and all of the king's men*
> *Couldn't put Humpty Dumpty back together again.*

Like Humpty Dumpty, we can't get up and dust ourselves off after the *Fall*. All of mankind, including God's entire *Creation*, is critically affected and utterly helpless to heal ourselves. Our *Fall* from glory did not just create *distance* between us and God, but also *depravity* in our hearts. As a result of the *Fall*, every aspect of our humanity, and God's creation, is in desperate need of restoration. *All things* are broken. And, just as we should pay careful attention to a trustworthy doctor when pursuing a correct diagnosis, we can only discover the great degree to which something is broken by listening to God speak to us in the Bible.

Most stories of redemption stop at the point where that which was lost, stolen, or forfeited is simply regained, returned, or replaced. Thus, lovers separated by war are reunited, or a widower marries his childhood sweetheart, or an irresponsible husband is restored to his forgiving wife.

But, as John shows us, the Bible's one Big Story includes a *fourth* element in its plot: *Consummation,* which is the element that separates the Bible from all other "stories of redemption." At this point, the plot doesn't get thick; it gets thrilling! In a sense, *Consummation* can be understood as "*Creation* on steroids." God has designed the ending of His Story to be even more wonderful than its beginning.

Redemption involves much more than a return to the way things were in *Creation*. Yes, it's *much* more fantastic. The *Redemption* we receive through the work of Jesus will enable us to realize the potential contained in *Creation*—which will only be fully realized at *Consummation!* Think of a magnificent rose bud (Creation) that became diseased (Fall) but is being healed (Redemption) and will one day reach full blossom (Consummation).

Therefore, *Redemption*, through the life, death, and resurrection of Jesus Christ . . .

(1) celebrates God's first *Creation*.

(2) sabotages the effects of the *Fall*.

(3) inaugurates the glories of *Consummation*.

The Bible's story of *Redemption* centers on Jesus. He is worshiped for *paying the great price* of our *Redemption* by His life, death, and resurrection. He is also honored as the one who *directs the whole process* of our *Redemption*. He is a King whose kingdom is a "reign of restoration," with the dominion of sovereign grace and power progressively making all things "new." All the king's horses and all the king's men may not be able to put *anything* or *anyone* back together again—but Jesus, their true King, can!

THE BIG FOUR

These four plot elements can be found woven throughout the Bible. But they virtually jump off the page in John's powerful account of the new world. "I saw a new heaven and a new earth, for the first heaven and the first earth had passed away, and there was no longer any sea" (Revelation 21:1).

CREATION—"the first heaven and the first earth"

The "first heaven and the first earth" references *Creation* (Genesis 1–2) as the starting point for understanding John's vision. He is intentional about placing his description of the new heaven and new earth in the context of the bigger story that God is telling through the whole Bible. John wants us to remember the *whole* DVD of God's Story as we get ready to experience the wonder of our future.

FALL—"there was no longer any sea"

Though it may seem a bit odd for John to describe something that is *not* present in the new world, this reference serves as both an important reminder and a wonderful affirmation. In Revelation, as in other parts of the Bible, the "sea" often stands for chaos, evil, restless insubordination, and opposition to the kingdom of God (Job 38:8-11; Psalm 89:9; Isaiah 57:20; Revelation 13:1). Thus, by emphasizing the absence of the sea, John is acknowledging both the historic reality and the tragic consequences of the *Fall*. But he is also celebrating the sabotaging of the *Fall* through the *Redemption* Jesus has accomplished. John is *not* suggesting (thank God) that there won't be any oceans or beaches in the new heaven and new earth.

REDEMPTION—"the first heaven and first earth had passed away"

The reference to the "passing away" of the first heaven and first earth celebrates the culmination of the long history of *Redemption*, and, therefore, it highlights God as the great Promise Keeper. After the *Fall*, God graciously revealed his promise for the restoration of His broken people (Genesis 3:15) and the renewal of His broken creation (Isaiah 65:17; 66:22). The story of *Redemption* unfolds progressively from the Old Testament through the New Testament, consuming all but the first and last two chapters of the entire Bible. Jesus Christ is the lead character in the history of *Redemption*.

CONSUMMATION—"I saw a new heaven and a new earth"

John's vision of a new heaven and a new earth brings us to the fulfillment and fullness of God's Story. *Consummation* is the revelation of the perfect world Jesus has won for us by His life, death, and resurrection—the world in which every semblance of sin, evil, death, and brokenness will be gone forever. The first heaven and first earth—long in the labor pains of childbirth—will experience the exhilaration of transformation, and not elimination through annihilation. Jesus is making "all things new," not replacing old things with new things. The Garden of Eden will become the Global-Garden City!

> What God starts He finishes. The last two chapters of Revelation reveal the consummation of creation, the end for which the created order was intended and designed—the omega-point that is the actualization of the potential that was contained, like a germ, in the alpha-seed. For the end was enclosed in the beginning like a promise; and the beginning is there in the end, that is its completion. The point is that what God begins He completes. . . . Therefore the new creation of Revelation must not be sundered from the original creation of Genesis. The connection is that of continuity and completion. . . . Thus, the paradise that was lost is regained, and regained to a transcendental degree, in Christ."[2]

In light of our study, what is the best way visually to represent the four plot elements of God's Story? I suggest the following arrangement. To place *Consummation* above *Creation* is to remind ourselves that God's Story is not taking us *back* to the Garden of Eden, but *forward* to a new heaven and new earth. How could we not get excited about this? Can you imagine a more glorious story with which to engage?

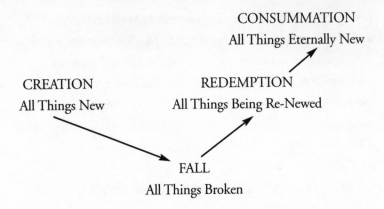

CONSUMMATION
All Things Eternally New

CREATION
All Things New

REDEMPTION
All Things Being Re-Newed

FALL
All Things Broken

Seek to become as familiar with this visualization of the four plot elements of God's Story as you possibly can. Seal it in your mind and heart. Let's learn to read any one part of the Bible, and each and every scene, with this restorative rhythm in mind. Think of different ways to trace this storyline through the Bible. Here are some examples:

A HORTICULTURAL INTERPRETATION

Tree of Life
in the New Heaven and New Earth

Tree of Life
in the Garden of Eden

Tree of Love
The Cross of Jesus

Tree of Loss
Sin Diseases Creation

A MUSICAL INTERPRETATION

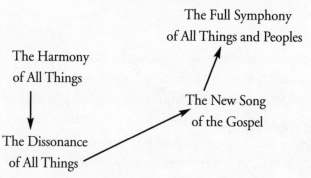

The Full Symphony
of All Things and Peoples

The Harmony
of All Things

The New Song
of the Gospel

The Dissonance
of All Things

A CULINARY INTERPRETATION

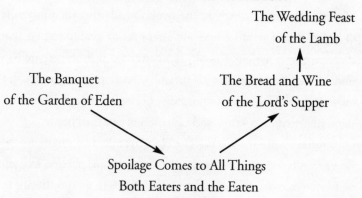

The Wedding Feast
of the Lamb

The Banquet
of the Garden of Eden

The Bread and Wine
of the Lord's Supper

Spoilage Comes to All Things
Both Eaters and the Eaten

This is God's Story. This is the story John knew backwards and forwards—the only story with the beauty and power to cause an eighty-year-old man living in exile to love Jesus with the passion and joy of a teenager. John chose not to waste away in the stadium seats of the Coliseum of Rome. He didn't criticize the coach's game plan from afar. He didn't keep score of others on the field. He "took actual snaps." And he is our model. Let's follow him as he followed Jesus.

FOR FURTHER REFLECTION

John's Creative Genius

To appreciate John's genius in crafting Revelation 21:1 as he did, consider this: of the 404 verses that comprise the twenty-two chapters of Revelation, 278 of them contain at least one reference to a passage in the Old Testament. John had a strong view of the importance and function of the Old Testament in the life of the early church. So what is the significance of this for us?

Like most artists and authors, John had definite purposes and goals in mind as he began writing Revelation. An artist's intent is often revealed most clearly in the symbols and other unique details of his writing. The more care and attention we give to recognizing these elements in John's book, the better we will be prepared to understand and experience his meaning. It's important to acquaint ourselves with his language and choice of symbols in order to understand his intent as a writer and his vision of our final home.

Think about it. What's the significance and challenge of Revelation being *saturated* with Old Testament prophecies, images, and references—references that John connects so specifically to Jesus? And what are the implications for you and me? Here's what occurs to me, and I encourage you to add to the list.

- John obviously had a high regard for the Old Testament Scriptures. He believed them to speak with the authority and voice of God.
- John trusted the Scriptures to be a trustworthy record of

God's creating and redeeming work in the world. John presents God as an active author-actor in His own Story.

- John wrote with the conviction that all of the promises of God—given during different periods and epochs in the history of redemption—were fulfilled in the life, death, and resurrection of Jesus.

- John knew himself to be both a *participant* and *proclaimer* of the one great story that the Bible tells through the old covenant promise and new covenant fulfillment.

- John wrote with an awareness that God's Story continued to unfold in the first-century church, and that it will continue to progress until all things He has promised are fulfilled at the return of Jesus. John expected all followers of Jesus to know and engage in this great story.

How Do *You* Think About the Bible?

Do we share John's convictions about the Bible? If pressed, how would you describe the essence and purpose of the Bible to a friend? Check out the following descriptions of what the Bible is and see if any match your view:

- A treasure chest full of promises waiting to be claimed by faith and that lead to a life of personal success, material wealth, and disease-free living.

- The Spirit-inspired record of the ways God has attempted to save His chosen people Israel—first through Moses, then through Jesus, and then by the creation of the Gentile church, whose existence will, in time, cause Israel to be jealous for God's love once again.

- God's Word brings personal revelation to each of us as the Holy Spirit creates fresh meanings from ancient texts.

- A book of commandments and religious rules tells us how to please God in the hopes of securing a place in heaven.

- A supernatural book, which if put in the glove compartment of your car, or carried in your shirt pocket, or placed somewhere in your children's bedroom, will keep evil and harm from coming near.

- A handbook for decoding anti-Christian conspiracy theories, recognizing the Antichrist, and preparing earnest Christians for the Rapture.

- A study of heroic leaders and commendable virtues that are the backbone of Western civilization and the foundation for American culture.

4 UNDERSTANDING BROKENNESS

"No one goes to the Grand Canyon to increase his self-esteem."
—JOHN PIPER

"Then the world was broken, fallen and battered and scarred
You took the hopeless, the life wasted,
ruined, and marred . . . and made it new
You turn winter into spring, You take every living thing
And You breathe the breath of life into it over and over again"
— SCC, "All Things New"

(SCOTTY):

By my racing heart, I could tell that either my ADD was kicking in or God's grace had brought a measure of longed-for freedom. Though all eight of us were adults, I felt like a first-grader excitedly preparing for show-and-tell at the beginning of the school year—a little insecure, but raring to go. This was our last time together as a group, before we parted company and headed for our homes, spread all over the country.

Our final assignment had been to draw symbols on a paper shield, indicating the warfare, victories, hopes, and dreams of our stories. We made it halfway around the circle, and it was finally my turn. "OK, you guys, I've never won an art show, but I'll gladly interpret my simple doodles for you."

Darlene and I were at the end of ten exhausting, but fruitful, days of heart work. Though described as a "marriage retreat," it felt more like we'd been on the set of *ER*. Surgeons, skilled in the ways of the soul, had been helping us identify the brokenness each of us brought into our marriage, and the ways we'd been sabotaging our communication and intimacy. Thirty years into our relationship, Darlene and I weren't about to give up, though, at times, the exposing power of marriage was much more than we ever bargained for.

As with most couples, God used marriage to reveal the wounds, the Samsonite baggage, and the idols we were carrying long before we met each other. Though it's hard for any of us to "own our stuff," it's our *stuff* that alone qualifies us for the healing and liberating grace of Jesus.

The marriage retreat began with three intense days of diagnostic interactions, assignments, and inventories, with the goal of identifying the main issues we needed to address—both as a couple and as individuals. Wisely, the leaders gave us Friday afternoon through Sunday evening to "chill out a little bit" and prepare for a full week of hard work.

Oh, we *chilled*—but it was more like the chill of a deep freezer than the chill of a comfortable recliner. Months in advance, I'd made reservations for us to visit the art colony of Sedona, Arizona, and then drive up to the Grand Canyon and spend the night. It was a good plan, but God's agenda for the trip proved to be different than mine—which wasn't a big surprise.

Still, there was no way I could've anticipated the emotional meltdown I was going to experience. Jesus knew it was time for me to *own* the sadness, self-pity, anger, and shame I'd been carrying around as a husband for way too long, and to acknowledge my powerlessness to do anything about it. Here's the way I described parts of the trip in my journal. The rawness of these words, and the obvious anguish I expressed, indicates how much I was like a can of Coke somebody shook up before popping the tab. I'm spewing, baby!

The climate inside our rental car mirrored the gray, dreary weather on the outside. I'd been so looking forward to visiting the Grand Canyon, but as we headed north with the radio off, an old Bob Bennett song came to mind— "Together All Alone." That's us—that's me, God. I've never felt more alienation and hopelessness.

It was as though the dam holding back the waters of the Colorado River at the north end of the canyon was beginning to fracture and leak from a duress no engineer could have anticipated or prevented. The emotional dam I built around my heart could no longer restrain years of suppressed hurt, unspoken fears, and my foolish strategies for hiding and pretending—all of which were now at flood-stage level in my marriage.

I strained to make sure I didn't miss or misread any of the highway signs, and provoke an even greater sense of shame and failure. All I could think about was getting lost in the desert, running out of gas, or puncturing a tire. Dad navigated huge ships to over sixty countries of the world, just by reading his sextant and God's stars. Why was I born such a direction dolt? Never has a three-hour drive felt more like three weeks. I felt myself getting more and more angry, and I'm not really sure why. I've never been in the car that long with Darlene with nothing being said between us.

Several tourist shops, cacti, and roadside elk sightings later, finally, we arrived. Driving through the large park entrance, I still felt lost as a goose. And to think, only a few months earlier, I'd marked this spot on my AAA travel map with a bright yellow smiley face.

I don't remember parking the car, but I do remember the awkward silence between us as we walked the path leading to the rim of the Grand Canyon. I wanted to grab Darlene's hand, but I feared her rejection more than I hoped for her touch.

As I stepped down onto the concrete viewing platform, I almost expected to hear a TV announcer voice shout over a loud speaker, "This is your life!" I felt the Grand Canyon more than I saw it. Forget national monuments or wonders of the world, I was looking at a plaster-cast mold of my insides—a geophysical sonogram of my guts. I hate feeling so empty, so cut off from Darlene, from myself, and from any sense of a future or hope . . .

About an hour later, my despair at least receded to acute sadness. The searing Arizona sun burned its way through the low-hanging, late-afternoon clouds. Like a laser paintbrush, the sun's rays splashed onto the surface on the canyon walls, creating an Aztec-colored rainbow—a reminder of one of God's oldest promises [Genesis 9:8–17]. At last, I did grab Darlene's hand, kind of by accident when I handed her a cup of hot tea—it was our first touch in hours. Her light squeeze was enough for the moment.

Thankfully, the drive back through the desert was much less tense. We reached a truce, probably out of sheer emotional exhaustion. Jesus, please turn this truce into trust.

BREAKTHROUGH AND THROUGH

Why did so much pain surface when we were supposed to be "chillin' out"? Because Jesus loves us like nobody else can or will. He came into the world to bind up the brokenhearted, to proclaim liberty for captives, to open prison doors for those who are bound, and to proclaim the year of the Lord's favor (Isaiah 61:1–2).

Getting free involves getting honest—brutally honest. We are prisoners needing God's favor and Jesus' deliverance. Only Jesus loves us enough to come to us in our captivities *and* confront us about our complicities. And only God's grace enables us to accept that we are victims bound by the damage of others, the result of living in a fallen world. But it also frees us to see how we are agents who bind others *and* ourselves, often wrapping chains around our own hearts and ankles.

The first three days of our retreat consisted of a frontal assault on my defense mechanisms, and a rude exposure of my foolish strategies for "surviving" marriage—that's right, *surviving* my own marriage. On the first day, I discovered I'd placed myself under the care of counselors over whom I had *no* control. Caregivers who didn't know me, my name, or my church from an eggplant. Professionals who were not the least bit enamored with my biblical knowledge, nor the veneer of my southern niceness. And I hate being out of control.

My main counselor (I'll call him Dave) helped me see the degree to which I entered marriage with a resolve to protect my heart against all shame and abandonment. In terms of seeking to build intimacy in marriage, that's sort of like saying, "Oh, there's my intimacy foot—I think I'll shoot it."

There were two assignments he gave me that proved to be quite helpful, if not painful. The first was briefly to write about my dating history, and the story of how Darlene and I met, courted, and got married. The assumption is that most of us are so busy living our stories that we don't take the necessary time to process and understand them—which is another way of saying that an unexamined life is a train wreck waiting to happen, just like an unexamined marriage. Here's a portion of what I wrote, synthesized with some of the insight I gained during the retreat.

My Marriage Story

I really wasn't looking to get involved with anyone when I met Darlene. In fact, I'd kind of declared a hiatus from dating for a while, as I needed to work on my grades a little. It was Saturday afternoon, and I was at a friend's house for a regular Bible study. Everything was normal—until Darlene came in through a side door. I'm not joking—if I'd been eating salad, I probably would have had a couple of spinach leaves hanging over my lip while drooling Thousand Island dressing.

She filled the room like a sunrise, wearing a canary-yellow jumpsuit and a dark Ocean Drive tan. With sun-streaked, shoulder-length hair, she was drop-dead gorgeous. Her cousin introduced us, but Darlene didn't give off any signs of wanting to chitchat. Later she told me that, for some reason, she thought I was already married.

As pretty as she was, watching the way she seemed to love God with abandon during the praise time and Bible study was just as attractive to me. When we met, she had only been a Christian two weeks. Two hours later, I was convinced Darlene Gale Eakin, one day, would be my wife. I was twenty, and she had just turned nineteen.

Eighteen months passed, and after a few friendly chats at Bible studies, a half-dozen or so "brotherly-sisterly-in-the-Lord" letters exchanged, it was time for me to make my move. Believing Darlene was out of my league (even though I thought we'd be married someday), I wanted to make sure, she wasn't currently dating anyone, and that she'd be inclined to respond positively, if I were to ask her out. So I had her first cousin, Sandy, run interference for me by checking the situation out. She gave me the green light.

Though I regularly dated and smooched my way through high school, I purposely stayed away from possessive-going-steady relationships—which says more about my control issues than it reflects wisdom. I was naïve as anyone could have been about their own heart and the meaning of marriage. Nevertheless, I concluded that Darlene was *perfect* for me: She was beautiful, spiritually on fire, "low-maintenance," and nonclingy. As bad as that sounds, in retrospect, I was probably hoping for part Geisha girl, Food

Channel cook, deaf-mute, spiritual giant, and independently wealthy nurse/carpenter.

So, still holding on to my first-meeting nuptial impression, I called Darlene in late December, 1971, and asked if I could come for a visit at her home in Greensboro, North Carolina. She made me a happy man by saying, "I'd love to see you." How I preened after that call.

My dating history was devoid of any post-romantic stress. Darlene wouldn't have to worry about this being a rebound relationship, because I'd never had any painful relationships from which to rebound. I'd never been rejected by a girlfriend—abandoned through death (both my mom and a girlfriend whom I casually dated off and on through high school were killed in car wrecks), but never heartbroken by a breakup. In fact, I didn't have any failed relationships in my first twenty-one years of life.

But it's hard to miss people in whom you have no heart investment. And for a relationship to have a chance at failing, a relationship has to exist. I lived as an orphan in my own home and like a visitor in somebody else's town—with neither roots nor connections.

After coming to faith in Jesus as a senior in high school, I began, unwittingly, to put a spiritual spin on my *intimacy-lite* way of relating to people. "My satisfaction and significance are in Jesus, not in people," I would boast. "I don't have time for deep relationships. I'm seeking to love Jesus with all my heart." I was sincere, but sincerely wrong.

My whirlwind courtship with Darlene consisted mostly of going to Bible studies and other "spiritual" gatherings. Though it didn't take long for us to become romantically involved, Darlene later confided that during our first date, she found my puns and corny sense of humor so irritating that she almost prayed I'd go on home. But providence prevailed, and, shortly thereafter, I sensed it was time to ask her to become my wife.

Not having a mom since the age of eleven and living in total disconnect from my dad, I was in the dark about many, many things—including proposal protocol and *little things* like engagement rings. So, not on bended knee, but sitting behind the steering wheel, driving along Interstate 85, I proposed . . . ringless and clueless.

What in the world made me think that I was ready for marriage as a twenty-two-year-old senior in college? And why did Darlene agree? Looking back, both of us agree we had three things in common: fractured families, wounded hearts, and a dangerously simplistic spirituality. Intuitively, we must have sensed that we were very much alike, or at least broken in familiar ways.

It was 1972, and we were a part of a generation that thought Jesus' second coming was imminent—quite likely by 1975. Why, therefore, should we spend much time building a normal friendship, processing our stories, or sharing dreams? Why invest in extended premarital counseling? Why expend energy on anything else than spiritual priorities and looking for the Apocalypse? So, after a three-month engagement, we celebrated our wedding on May 5, 1972. Needless to say, Jesus didn't come back in 1975, and we have cried out many times since, "How long, O Lord?"

Bad Tapes

The second assignment Dave gave me was to make a list of the "tapes," or reoccurring messages, that have been the subliminal soundtrack for my life—like the unwanted Muzak you find yourself humming at the most unsuspecting times. Here's the list I wrote out:

> You're on your own.
> Protect your heart.
> Buck up!
> You can be abandoned again in a second.
> Your opinions don't matter.
> Stay in control.
> Anger is dangerous.
> Outsmart them.
> Something's wrong with your body.
> Stay busy.
> All you have to offer is your giftedness.
> Avoid conflict at all costs.
> Most men can do things you can't.
> You're the Wizard of Oz.

Where did these messages come from? From as many sources as you can imagine: my parents, the devil, friends, coaches, the world, teachers, but mostly from a heart allergic to grace and committed to self-sufficiency (the essence of all idolatry).

I'm not sure how I expected Dave to respond to my list, but he sure didn't give me pity. It was more like, "You're better than that, Scotty, aren't you? So what's the payoff for holding onto these messages?" He knew I didn't need consolation, though my body language was probably screaming for it.

It wasn't as though I made a CD of these messages for cruising around in the car, anymore than Darlene worked up a dance routine to hers. But these thoughts became fair game for Satan to exploit as Darlene and I moved from the innocence of our first weeks of marriage into the intensity of sharing our lives together. The ink wasn't even dry on this list as we were packing our overnight bags for our "chillin' out" weekend.

BROKEN AND BROKENNESS

Considering how much of my *stuff* was revealed in these two assignments, it's pretty easy to see why I hit the wall emotionally. The closer we got to the Grand Canyon, the more time I had to think about the things Dave brought to light—especially with Darlene sitting eighteen inches away in the front seat. (She was pretty raw from the rigors of her first three days as well.) Only God knew that a burned-out former pastor would be the perfect vehicle to corner me, redemptively. I had *zero* control over this man, and that's just as it needed to be. He read me like a flashing neon sign, and we both knew it.

Every time I see a picture of the Grand Canyon now, or even hear it named, my knees get a little weak. I'll always remember how God used the "brokenness" of that enormous chasm to help me connect with my own brokenness. And that's exactly what that gigantic hole in the ground is—a broken portion of God's magnificent creation. Precious terra firma, ravaged by years of erosion, sandblasting windstorms, and the ruthless power of the desert sun.

Every place and every thing Jesus created is broken. *Nothing* is today as it was meant to be in the beginning. The beauty of the Grand Canyon today is just an echo of the greater beauty the same piece of real estate manifested before sin and death entered Creation. Likewise, the holes in my heart, and the multiple layers of decaying sediment in my marriage, bore testimony to the ravaging effects of sin, death, and life in a fallen world.

I was able to mask and micromanage my brokenness for a long time, but ignored wounds, mismanaged emotions, and idols of the heart inevitably caught up with me. Marriage has more power than *any* other human relationship to reveal both our dignity and depravity, and our beauty and our brokenness. There simply aren't many places to hide—or, at least, for very long.

But Jesus doesn't draw attention to the broken places in our lives to *humiliate* us, but to *humble* us and to *heal* us. He gives *grace* to the humble, and not *grades*. As Darlene and I watched the sun transfigure layers of decaying sediment into kaleidoscopic art, I got a tiny glimpse of the *beauty of brokenness*—a glimpse that grew to a gaze the next week. Jesus shines the light of the gospel on us both to *expose our brokenness* (revealing the broken places in our lives) and to *bring us to brokenness* (to honesty, humility, and repentance).

I guess we should call this *gospel brokenness*, because only the gospel of God's grace can enable us to be completely honest about our stuff without falling into toxic shame or self-contempt. And only the gospel can humble us, soften us, and give us the power to repent—or, at least, not run away or rant. When followers of Jesus walk openly in this kind of brokenness—*gospel brokenness*—angels in heaven rejoice, and people without faith, or those with much cynicism about Christians, are likely to reconsider who Jesus is.

Write this down: no greater beauty can be found at *any point* or in *any place* in God's Story than the times when God's people manifest this *gospel brokenness*—for that's where God's glory is revealed most clearly. What does this kind of brokenness look like?

A notoriously sinful woman shamelessly enters the home of a scorning Pharisee to wash the feet of Jesus with her tress and tears. She is filled with adoration and astonishment, for Jesus welcomed her and washed her heart with His lavish grace. She loves Him extravagantly because she was forgiven extravagantly (Luke 7:36–50).

A rebellious, now broken and broke son returns to his father's home with sorrow and humility, but without excuses or promises. To his amazement, his father runs to greet him, and then brings him onto the dance floor of mercy and fetes him with the fatted calf of grace (Luke 15:11–32).

A promiscuous woman, who was guilty of sequential affairs, receives living water from Jesus. Then, she drops everything and risks all to invite the men and women of her Samaritan community "to come and see the One who told me everything I ever did." Her story of prostitution is absorbed into His story of restoration (John 4:5–42).

A self-righteous Pharisee, bigot, and murderer is struck blind so that he might see the beauty of Jesus and receive the immeasurable riches of His sovereign grace. His arrogance gives way to apostleship, and Paul's story becomes sweeter as he grows older. Only gospel brokenness can free a proud man to proclaim, "Christ Jesus came into the world to save sinners, of whom I am the foremost. But I received mercy for this reason, that in me, as the foremost, Jesus Christ might display his perfect patience as an example to those who were to believe in him for eternal life" (1 Timothy 1:15–16).

BABY STEPS IN GOSPEL BROKENNESS

Darlene and I returned from the Grand Canyon in time for a Sunday evening meeting designed to help everyone re-enter retreat mode. Our grueling schedule began bright and early on Monday morning with a regimen of small-group exercises, individual work, couple work, journaling, and prayer—the combination of which Jesus used in powerful ways. By God's sheer generosity, we saw what the beauty of gospel brokenness can look like in marriage—specifically, in *our* marriage.

We began with baby steps—not metaphorical baby steps, but literal ones. The most important thing we worked on during our retreat was our communication, and we did so using "baby steps" around two canvas mats designed to help couples give each other feedback lovingly and receive feedback nondefensively.

COMMUNICATION BREAKTHROUGH

As clumsy as we were in using the mats at first (it was kind of like playing twister), it was a whole lot more enjoyable than the *wrestling* mat we'd been on previously. For one thing, we were forced into a much slower speaking and listening process.

I learned to speak for myself, and to let Darlene do the same without interrupting or rewriting her messages, and vice versa. I began to hear the difference between what she was saying and what she was feeling. The more we practiced, the more it felt like we were citizens of two different countries learning a third exciting language together. Our walls and defenses started to crumble, and a bridge began to emerge.

Nothing was more obviously broken in our thirty-year-old marriage than our communication. Neither of us experienced healthy communication patterns in our homes, nor were we given the tools anywhere else to know how to handle conflict redemptively. Generally speaking, Darlene came from a home in which getting loud and large, or withdrawing into a prolonged, rejecting silence, were both used as strategies for dealing with disappointment and disagreements.

In my home, we were all basically conflict avoidant. I don't have a single memory of my parents ever having a disagreement, or even expressing irritation with one another. But, neither do I have one memory of my mom, dad, brother, and me sitting together to share opinions, process an issue, or even have a conversation. And after Mom died, my dad, brother, and I each basically went our own separate ways—internalizing the very things that needed to be expressed and isolating ourselves at the time we needed community the most.

So when Darlene and I got married, we brought all these different pieces of broken communication baggage with us. To make matters worse, we were both trying to live up to the standards of a performance-based *superspirituality*, which led us to believe that if you *really* married in God's will, then you and your spouse would agree about all things. And you certainly wouldn't have fights.

To survive all this baggage, brokenness, and spiritual bravado, *denial* and *control* took root in our communication. We *denied* feelings that seemed to threaten the harmony of marriage and the thrust of God's commands, as we understood them. We (especially me) simply didn't know how to deal with our disappointments and differences, and the emotions of anger, sadness, fear, and doubt. Our theology didn't make room for these messy feelings. More faith, and more of the Holy Spirit, were supposed to eliminate these feelings—right? To use Brennan Manning's term, we kept "should-ing all over ourselves"—"A good Christian shouldn't oughta feel this way." I (now, thankfully) get angry and sad when I look back at the way that bad teaching filled our wounded hearts and made it so easy for us to relate to each other so contrary to the freedom of the gospel.

I used *control* to minimize our differences in an effort to sustain "peace" and tranquility in our marriage. Not having a particularly powerful personality, I'd easily resort to my default mode of teaching and explaining as the primary way of keeping equilibrium in our relationship. That translated into living from my head a lot more than from my heart. Any intensity in our relationship fueled fears of abandonment in me. But in light of Darlene's life story, to feel controlled translated into being devalued. The dance between my fear of abandonment and her fear of devaluation persisted for years, and it paralyzed our communication. (This was a *huge* theme that surfaced during our time in Arizona.)

Fortunately, in time, we did break away from the legalism and bad teaching in which we began our marriage. We came to understand and experience that God accepts us, and continues to love us, not because of anything *we* do, but because of Jesus' finished work on the Cross—plus nothing.

But restoration is a long, healing journey in the same direction—a journey that begins most powerfully at the intersection of God's grace and our specific brokenness. Our broken communication ruts were about as deep as the Grand Canyon itself. That's why from day one, and continuing throughout the rest of the retreat, our counselors put us on "the mats." We spent *a lot* of time on the mats!

WE'VE ONLY JUST BEGUN

Time on the mats and more intense work and reflection helped us identify ways that we'd been sabotaging our intimacy. For me, that involved several important things. Though, in recent years, I had finally begun to grieve my mom's death—and as a result, deeply connect with my dad—I had to face this reality: for more than a quarter-of-a-century of our marriage, Darlene lived with an emotionally ambivalent husband.

As a result, I needed to understand, among other things, the price Darlene paid for my sinful strategies in dealing with my loss and pain—my passive aggressiveness, busyness, withdrawal into silence, too many words and too little emotion, which were all my control idols.

But, I didn't just need a list of the ways I loved her poorly; I needed to grieve these things before the throne of grace and before Darlene. I had to repent and submit to Jesus' restoring work. At this point, the beauty of gospel brokenness began to show up in our marriage. While Jesus was busy showing me *my* broken places and taking me to broken-ness, He was doing the same thing in Darlene's heart. As I began to own my *stuff,* Jesus was enabling Darlene to own hers. We began to see ourselves less as victims of each other's *stuff* and more as individuals called to take responsibility for ourselves and for our responses.

Describing the joy of moving toward each other in humility, gentleness, and strength is like trying to describe your first kiss or the birth of one of your children. We're learning to forgive from the heart; process issues with girt and grace, and not with denial and control; speak for ourselves clearly, and listen to each other deeply; accept each other's weaknesses without trying to fix each other; be honest about our disappointments; fight fair without having to win; honor each other as individuals; heal old wounds; repent quicker; eliminate labels; dream about our future together; and come to the Cross together.

I am not suggesting we've arrived at some place of perfection in our marriage—*far* from it. What Jesus has done for us is to demonstrate that His name, indeed, *is* Redeemer. He *has* come to restore broken things, and, by His grace, we've been able to admit that we're two broken individuals—with a broken marriage and broken communication, in desperate need of what Jesus alone can give. Though we've been married for thirty-three years, we feel like babies in the journey of intimacy and grateful that Jesus has come to make all things new. It may be cliché, but if Jesus can work in our marriage, then He can work in yours.

FOR FURTHER REFLECTION

Understanding the Relationship Between Broken and Brokenness
Because the language of *brokenness* is used in so many different ways, I hope the following section will clarify this important concept. There are two types of *brokenness* that we need to understand and experience, both of which are vital to God's Story and to the process of restoration. Let's call them *Brokenness A* and *B*. To illustrate both of them, we'll use the biblical theme of "the heart."

Definition of *Brokenness A:* Something is *broken* to the degree it doesn't reveal God's glory and serve the purposes of His Story.

Explanation: God created our hearts for loving Him as He deserves and demands—with our thoughts, emotions, and choices. Therefore, our hearts are *Broken A* to the extent that they don't think the thoughts of God, desire the things of God, and choose the will of God.

- "The LORD saw how great man's wickedness on the earth had become, and that every inclination of *the thoughts of his heart was only evil all the time*" (Genesis 6:5 NIV, emphasis mine).

- "*The heart is deceitful above all things* and beyond cure. Who can understand it?" (Jeremiah 17:9 NIV, emphasis mine).

- "And the LORD said: 'Because this people draw near with their mouth and honor me with their lips, while *their hearts are far from me*'" (Isaiah 29:13, emphasis mine).

- "*Their heart is false;* now they must bear their guilt" (Hosea 10:2).

- "But this people has *a stubborn and rebellious heart*; they have turned aside and gone away" (Jeremiah 5:23, emphasis mine).

Example: The main image Scripture uses to demonstrate *Brokenness A* is idolatry or false worship—that is, giving anything or anyone the adoration, attention, allegiance, and affection of which Jesus alone is worthy. Paul describes a "broken heart" as one which has "exchanged the truth of God for a lie, and worshiped and served created things rather than the Creator—who is forever praised. Amen" (Romans 1:25, NIV). Therefore, *Brokenness A* is a worship disorder.

Definition of *Brokenness B*: An attitude of contrition, humility, and repentance in response to the specific ways we don't reveal God's glory.

Explanation: Our hearts were created for loving God as He deserves and demands—with our thoughts, emotions, and choices. Therefore, we are *Broken B* to the extent we are convicted, humbled, and repentant for the specific ways we don't love God with our mind, heart, and will.

- "The sacrifices of God are a broken spirit; a broken and contrite heart, O God, you will not despise" (Psalm 51:17, NIV).

Example: One of the most well-known examples of *Brokenness B* is found in the story of the Prodigal Son (Luke 15). The younger son demonstrated *Brokenness B* when he "came to his senses," and began to grieve over the way he sinned against his loving father; then, he humbled himself and returned home as a repentant son.

Another way to connect with *Brokenness B* is to think of Jesus as a great horse trainer breaking a wild, independent bucking bronco. He intends to tame us, and not to harm us. The goal of brokenness is to bring us to a humble, submissive spirit, and not to self-contempt and fearful compliance.

To become a character and carrier of God's Story requires us to engage with both *Brokenness A* and *B:* we need Jesus to show us the ways we are broken *(A)* *and* to bring us to brokenness *(B)*.

THE MEANING OF "BROKEN"

Something is broken if it contradicts God's original design, present purposes, and future plans. As Creator and Re-Creator, only Jesus has the right to say when something is healthy or broken.

Remember, "broken" is not a category of pragmatism (How do we fix broken things for *our* benefit?), but a calling to praise (How do we deal with the broken things for *God's* glory?). A relationship isn't necessarily broken just because it doesn't work the way we think it should—that is, when it doesn't make us happy or "fill us up." A relationship, or anything else, is broken when it doesn't worship God—that is, when it doesn't serve the purpose of God's Story and "fill the universe" with the glory of Jesus (Ephesians 4:7–10).

THE MEANING OF "BROKENNESS"

"Brokenness" is a humble and contrite spirit as created by the Holy Spirit when we "see" and grieve the specific ways we contradict God's original design, present purposes, and future goals. It's vastly different from "broken-down-ness." The discrepancy stems from what the Bible calls "godly sorrow" and "worldly sorrow" (2 Corinthians 7:8–11). Godly sorrow brings change, healing, and freedom from regret. Worldly sorrow only brings the stench of death—the decaying aroma of self-righteousness, self-pity, self-delusion, self-preoccupation, and self-contempt.

5 RESTORING GOD'S BROKEN CREATION

"God doesn't make junk and He will not junk what He has made."
—ALBERT WOLTERS

"You spoke and made the sunrise to light up the very first day
You breathed across the water and started the very first wave
It was You . . . You introduced Your glory to
every living creature on earth
And they started singing the first song to ever be heard . . .
They sang for You"
— SCC, "All Things New"

(SCOTTY):

The retreat was just a few hours from being over. All of us were encouraged but understandably exhausted and ready to get home. By no means had this been the kind of retreat that ends with everybody singing campfire songs, eating s'mores, and posing for the group photo. It'd been intense, but immensely important for all of us. Our final small-group gathering gave each of us a chance to share our hearts and hopes.

"Can everybody see OK?" I held up my paper shield and proceeded to explain what my little stick-men sketches and symbols conveyed.

"This first symbol is a fractured heart in a lock-box with the lid torn off. This week, I've been learning to accept my weakness and brokenness without needing to hide behind excuses or explanations . . . or the illusion that there's a safe place I can keep my heart from ever hurting again. The lock-box has been trashed. I'm leaving this place acutely aware of how much of God's grace I will need to live as a free man, especially as a husband. And that's my longing.

"Next . . . my grandmother used to make awesome fig preserves from figs grown in her backyard, so I thought I remembered what fig leaves look like. But these three things hanging from a clothes rack, in case you can't tell, look more like the leaf on the Canadian flag. I guess that would make them maple leaves. Oh well, these leaves represent three of the foolish ways I've been trying to hide from God and Darlene in my marriage: busyness, theology, and self-contempt.

"Going home, I'm determined to repent of living life at a pace that's made it easy for me to ignore the voice of God and the cries of my wife. I've used the excuse of vocational ministry to ignore my idol of busyness. Second leaf, I'm committed to learn how to live less from the information crammed in my head and more from my heart. If my theology doesn't make me more present in my marriage, then I've either got the wrong theology, or my theology is right, but I don't really believe it. Last fig leaf . . . I've realized this week how quickly I go to shame and self-contempt as a way of numbing myself to the demands of relationships. But self-pity sabotages intimacy as much as megalomania does. Whatever kind of leaves these are, I want them, by God's grace, off my back and out of my closet.

"Lastly, though it looks more like a shark, this is supposed to be Flipper, who is the dolphin equivalent of Lassie for my generation.

For as long as I can remember, Darlene has dreamed out loud about swimming with dolphins—somewhere, somehow. Well, the two little stick-people swimmers splashing and smiling around Flipper are us. I want to share that experience *with* you. I want to be less of a lone ranger in our marriage and more of a partner. We'll find dolphins to swim with, and then we'll get another dream."

APPREHENDING THE EMPEROR

After quite a bit of research, it became obvious that the best place to experience the dolphin world is Discovery Cove, in Sea World—one of many outstanding Disney adventures in Orlando, Florida. I made reservations for what is called "Dolphin Trainer for a Day"—a day-long experience of being immersed (quite literally) in the world of dolphins: their culture, habits, socialization, care, training, birthing, and early "childhood" experiences.

My first editor told me a writer should never say, "Words fail me." Well, mine do, so I'll let C. S. Lewis speak for me: "In order that we finite beings may apprehend the Emperor, He translates His glory into multiple forms—into stars, woods, waters, beasts, and the bodies of men [and dolphin]. Because God created the natural—invented it out of His love and artistry—it demands our reverence."[1]

"Apprehend the Emperor" . . . I love that phrase because it captures the essence of God's Story. God delights to make Himself known, and He does so with the greatest of joy through the things He has made. Twelve hours of connecting with dolphins brought a new dimension and splendor to three decades of Bible study. Please don't misunderstand me and charge me with pantheism (violating the first two of the Ten Commandments), or with Sea World idolatry. But a day spent with grinning, fun-loving dolphins—with more personality than most Christians I know—gave me a clearer glimpse of the God who smiles. What other emperor would dare to take credit for the playfulness, tenderness, and brilliance of a dolphin?

Is God really this passionate and involved with the things he has made? Does He actually delight in His creation? If you doubt it, just take the time to wrestle with the questions God put to Job: "Where were you when I laid the earth's foundation? Tell me, if you understand. Who marked off its dimensions? Surely you know! Who stretched a measuring line across it? On what were its footings set, or who laid its cornerstone—while the morning stars sang together and all the angels shouted for joy?" (Job 38:4–7 NIV).

Astonishing! According to this Scripture, even before there were men to sing, God made singing stars and shouting angels filled with his joy. The Fall may have muffled the song, but it could never mute creation's joyful proclamation of God's glory. Well after sin polluted every sphere of creation, King David pronounced, "The heavens declare the glory of God; the skies proclaim the work of his hands. Day after day they pour forth speech; night after night they display knowledge. There is no speech or language where their voice is not heard" (Psalm 19:1–3 NIV). There is *no place* in the universe where creation is not singing God's praise.

From Sea Hunt to Sea World

While we were putting on our black rubber wetsuits, the official *"uni"* for Discovery Cove guests, I remembered one of my favorite afternoon TV programs that I watched every afternoon as a kid. *Sea Hunt* chronicled the adventures of scuba diver Mike Nelson, as played by Lloyd Bridges. I used to dream of fighting off sharks and giant octopi while rescuing stranded fishermen. But those heroic imaginings were quickly supplanted by the fulfilling of a dream of far greater significance—Darlene's.

We learned so much about dolphins—and, therefore, about their glorious Creator. Here are just a few tidbits I'll never forget. Of all mammals, only dolphin babies, or calves, are born tail first. And, once born, they stay close to their mothers for two or three years. Soon after birth, another female dolphin comes alongside of mother and baby to serve as a nursemaid, or "auntie," until the calf is mature enough to separate from its mother.

Their dorsal fins are just as distinctive as our faces, and each dolphin has its own signature whistle that distinguishes it from all other dolphins, much like our fingerprints. Lifelong bonding between individual dolphins occurs frequently. They're known to care for sick and dying members of their pod, or family group, and, when danger is nearby, they work together to protect one another.

At the end of the day, I couldn't help but think how great it would be if we—human mammals—demonstrated more of the loyalty, community, and care that dolphins have. Then something else occurred to me. To have traveled with Darlene from the grueling moments and painful disconnect we experienced at the Grand Canyon into the firstfruits of fresh renewal in our hearts and marriage, and to have just shared a day in childlike wonder, laughter, and joy: being pulled through the water while holding onto the dorsal fin of a dolphin; petting sting rays like they were puppies; feeding four-feet long nurse sharks behaving as though they were four-year-olds clamoring for vanilla wafers and apple juice; having exotic birds of all colors landing on our heads and eating out of our hands.

Though there was no praise band, Bible study, corporate prayer, kneeling, or sacraments, the whole day was full of worship. Only hearts hardened to God's glory and grace could resist acknowledging His unparalleled worth as revealed in the things we experienced at Discovery Cove. And to think, this was a tiny part of everyday life for Adam and Eve in the Garden of Eden, when nothing was broken and every relationship in the created universe was aligned and ordered for synergistic beauty and doxology—whole, healthy, and peaceful.

BETTER BY FAR

And yet, though hard to imagine or believe, as magnificent as life was for Adam and Eve before the Fall, the life yet to come—described in Revelation 21–22—will be greater *by far*. The consummate riches of the all-things-new world will make *everything* that has previously existed seem like a title page and introduction. Isaiah spoke of this renewed world with tantalizing images:

> The wolf shall dwell with the lamb, and the leopard shall lie down with the young goat, and the calf and the lion and the fattened calf together; and a little child shall lead them. The cow and the bear shall graze; their young shall lie down together; and the lion shall eat straw like the ox. The nursing child shall play over the hole of the cobra, and the weaned child shall put his hand on the

adder's den. They shall not hurt or destroy in all my holy
mountain; for the earth shall be full of the knowledge of
the LORD as the waters cover the sea (Isaiah 11:6–9).

We mustn't treat these words as mere poetry, but as prophecy to be
fulfilled in Jesus. Isaiah surveyed and savored the gargantuan implications of the Messiah's work from afar. Let's consider a few elements of
his deeply encouraging portrayal of the "world without end," and
how Jesus alone can bring these things to pass.

Against the backdrop of a forest leveled by God's judgment,
Isaiah described the arrival of the promised Messiah as a small
shoot emerging from a cut-off stump that is springing up to bring
new life to God's desolate creation and people (Isaiah 11:1). The
theme of greatness out of weakness, and vitality flowing from
humility, saturates the prophet's vision. "Today in the town of
David a Savior has been born to you; he is Christ the Lord. This
will be a sign to you: You will find a baby wrapped in cloths and
lying in a manger" (Luke 2:11–12 NIV).

And like redemptive kudzu, nothing will impede the consuming
growth of the True Vine. He will bear lush fruit in every place. "For
to us a child is born, to us a son is given; and the government shall
be upon His shoulder. . . . Of the increase of his government and of
peace there will be no end (Isaiah 9:6–7). His peace will eradicate
the dissonance and division brought into the world through sin.

The enmity between the woman's seed and the serpent will be
gone forever (Genesis 3:15). Old hostilities and *all* enmities will be
destroyed by the Messiah. "He himself is our peace, who has made
the two one and has destroyed the barrier, the dividing wall of

hostility" (Ephesians 2:14 NIV). Though he didn't know His name, it was Jesus whom Isaiah was speaking about in describing the day when God would fulfill His promise to crush the head of the serpent's seed and lift the judicial curse from all of creation (Genesis 3:15–19). "Christ redeemed us from the curse of the law by becoming a curse for us—for it is written, 'Cursed is everyone who is hanged on a tree'" (Galatians 3:13). "No longer will there be any curse" (Revelation 22:3 NIV).

All broken relationships will be replaced with reconciled and perfected ones—between God and man, neighbors and nations, man and beast, and also between predators and prey. Infants and weaned children will have nothing to fear from poisonous cobra and deadly vipers. Wolves will play with lambs, goats will cuddle with leopards, and lions will enjoy fattened calves without eating them.

Prejudice and racism in all forms and expressions will be gone. Cows and bears will live in the same neighborhood and send their children to the same schools. Imagine lion and ox eating straw together at the same restaurants—demonstrating the power of the Messiah to transform our natures and appetite. Tending and filling the new earth to God's glory will be the privilege of the childlike. "'Who is the greatest in the kingdom of heaven?' And calling to Him a child, he put him in the midst of them. . . . 'Whoever humbles himself like this child is the greatest in the kingdom of heaven'" (Matthew 18:1–2, 4).

Zion will no longer describe one holy mountain; but the entire earth will be filled with the presence, glory, and adoration of God. "Knowing the Lord" will be to the new world as water is to an ocean—total permeation!

A VARIED CHOIR

After our experience at Discovery Cove—after three extra days of enjoying all kinds of exhibits, performances of "playful" killer whales, and interacting with a *variety* of aquatic creatures living in the Sea World complex (including the baby dolphin nursery)—I read John's description of the restored world gathered like a massive choir in a brand-new way. "And I heard every creature in heaven and on earth and under the earth and in the sea, and all that is in them, saying, 'To him who sits on the throne and to the Lamb be blessing and honor and glory and might forever and ever!'" (Revelation 5:13).

Oh, for the day when we will hear every person, plant, porpoise, pine tree, and porcupine offering praise to the Creator and Re-Creator of all things, Jesus, the Lamb of God. John's pan-creation celebration reminds me of Walt Disney's movie, *Fantasia*, which depicts a wide array of creatures dancing to Tchaikovsky's "Nutcracker Suite." Whether he acknowledged it or not, the true source of Walt Disney's fascination with creation and childlikeness, and his love for the world of animals and family adventures, was God's Story. As Paul writes, "For His [God's] invisible attributes, namely, his eternal power and divine nature, have been clearly perceived, ever since the creation of the world, in the things that have been made" (Romans 1:20).

A small taste of this coming world of cosmic peace and transformed creation made Darlene and me hungry for more. And it's raised an important question: how would Jesus have us live in *this* world as we hear the echoes of the Garden of Eden, and get increasingly nostalgic for the Global-Garden-City of the new heaven and new earth? The question isn't, "Should we join Green Peace, P.E.T.A., or some other radical environmental group, *and* become vegetarians?" Rather, "As those who will inherit the earth, how do we live as stewards of it now, to the glory of God and the praise of Jesus?"

LEFT BEHIND OR LEFT OUT?

Many Christians pine for the day when they will *escape* the darkness of this world to be with the Lord in the glories of the next world. But God's Story calls us to be with the Lord *in this broken world*, as agents of transforming hope. Indeed, the gospel of God's grace liberates us to invest in Jesus' agenda for cosmic restoration, while it simultaneously intensifies our longings for the new heaven and new earth. Followers of Jesus are to live in the middle of God's fallen creation as resident aliens and servant sojourners. But what does this gospel-driven lifestyle look like?

It starts with our being certain about what *broken things* are included in the *all things* Jesus has committed to make new. Many Christians assume Jesus is only interested in "spiritual things," and that He disregards, if not disdains, "secular things." This leads to an invisible, but powerful, line (functionally, an impregnable *wall*), being drawn between "the things of the Lord" and "the things of the world."

We are exhorted by the line-drawers to invest our time, money, and energy in "the things of the Lord," and to have less and less to do with "the things of the world." The line is drawn at different places by different groups of Christians, but here is a general idea of how this bifurcation of life and creation often gets translated.

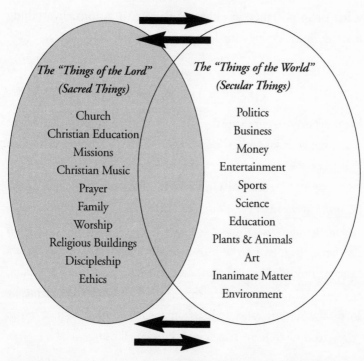

The "Things of the Lord"
(Sacred Things)

Church
Christian Education
Missions
Christian Music
Prayer
Family
Worship
Religious Buildings
Discipleship
Ethics

The "Things of the World"
(Secular Things)

Politics
Business
Money
Entertainment
Sports
Science
Education
Plants & Animals
Art
Inanimate Matter
Environment

But the Scriptures don't support this arbitrary division. God's Story affirms our Lord's love for *everything* He has designed and created: the animate and the inanimate, social structures and family units, the creative arts and the management of culture, the governance of life and the joys of leisure. God's cosmic delight with creation is established by the first two and last two chapters of the Bible.

God begins His Word with the creation of a heaven and earth (Genesis 1–2) and ends it with the re-creation of a new heaven and earth (Revelation 21–22). In neither of these accounts do we see anything that remotely suggests a division between "the things of the Lord" and "the things of the world." There is no hierarchy of value or importance in either of these two visions. Everything matters, and all things are done to the glory of God.

DRAWING THE RIGHT LINE

We don't need to eliminate the line; we just need to put it in the right place, between kingdoms, not categories. God's Story reveals a line that has been drawn between two *dominions*, and two antithetical reigns—the kingdom of God and the kingdom of Satan—both claiming authority over *all things*. There are no neutral areas in life and no demilitarized zones. *Every* sphere and aspect of God's creation has been invaded by the power of sin and death. *All things* are broken, and *all things* are contested. But Jesus has come to reclaim, redeem, and restore *all things* for the glory of God—and rightfully so, for the Scriptures herald Jesus' unique relationship with *all things*.

According to John 1:1–3, Jesus created all things:

> In the beginning was the Word, and the Word was with God, and the Word was God. He was in the beginning with God. All things were made through him, and without him was not any thing made that was made.

Jesus existed before all things, sustains all things, and is the goal of all things.

> For by him all things were created, in heaven and on earth, visible and invisible, whether thrones or dominions or rulers or authorities—all things were created through

him and for him. And he is before all things, and in him all things hold together (Colossians 1:16–17).

Jesus is the means by which all things—including ourselves—exist.

For us there is one God, the Father, from whom are all things and for whom we exist, and one Lord, Jesus Christ, through whom are all things and through whom we exist (1 Corinthians 8:6).

Jesus is the heir of all things.

Long ago, at many times and in many ways, God spoke to our fathers by the prophets, but in these last days he has spoken to us by his Son, whom he appointed the heir of all things, through whom also he created the world" (Hebrews 1:1–2).

Jesus is the final summation and unification of all things.

In him [Jesus] we have redemption through his blood, the forgiveness of our trespasses, according to the riches of His grace, which He lavished upon us, in all wisdom and insight making known to us the mystery of His will, according to His purpose, which He set forth in Christ as a plan for the fullness of time, to unite all things in him, things in heaven and things on earth (Ephesians 1:7–10).

New Testament scholar Oscar Cullmann created an effective illustration that explains the present conflict between Jesus and Satan, and between the kingdom of God and the kingdom of darkness. The two most significant days in the history of World War II are used to explain "the already and the not yet" of the redeeming work of Jesus.

The Second World War was essentially won on D-Day, when the Allied forces invaded the enemy's territory and established a base of operations, or a bridgehead. D-Day was "pregnant" with the certain victory of V-Day. Though the outcome of the war was secured at D-Day, there were many more battles and wartime casualties until V-Day arrived several months later.

In God's Story, the first coming of Christ was the equivalent of D-Day. Satan and the powers of darkness were substantially defeated, and victory over sin and death was secured by Jesus' death and resurrection.

> The reason the Son of God appeared was to destroy the works of the devil (1 John 3:8).

> Since therefore the children share in flesh and blood, He [Jesus] himself likewise partook of the same things, that through death He might destroy the one who has the power of death, that is, the devil, and deliver all those who through fear of death were subject to lifelong slavery (Hebrews 2:14–15).

> He [Jesus] disarmed the rulers and authorities and put them to open shame, by triumphing over them in him (Colossians 2:15).

At His second coming, or V-Day, the fullness of Jesus' victory will be manifest and celebrated forever in the perfections of the new heaven and new earth. But as in World War II, life between D-Day and V-Day still entails conflict and many battles for followers of Jesus. Our enemy, Satan, and his minions have been defeated, but not annihilated. And though the power of sin and death has been broken, it has not been eradicated.

We live, therefore, in the overlap of two dominions or eras. Like the Allies, during the Second World War, we are dealing with a dethroned foe not ready to concede defeat. Knowing his days are short, he is filled with fury, and will do *anything* possible to bring discouragement and harm to God's people en route to his own demise.

Think of a dispute between two kingdoms with two sovereigns who contend for the same territory and who lead two opposing armies into the field. Each army owes allegiance to one of the sovereigns. The territory in dispute, the creation of God, has been invaded by God's adversary, Satan, who now holds creation as an occupied territory with military force.

In Jesus Christ, God launches a counter-offensive to reclaim his rightful domain. By the death and resurrection of Jesus Christ, the victory has, in principle, been achieved. God has established a beachhead in creation and has staked out his claim for the whole. We now live in the period between the decisive battle won by Christ, and the definitive establishment of his sovereignty over all of his territories. The warfare that still rages between the soldiers of Christ and the agents of Satan has the character of a mop-up operation.[2]

We live in "the already and not yet" of Jesus' commitment to make all things new: in the "already" present reality and implications of Jesus' decisive victory over Satan, sin, and death, but also in the "not yet-ness" of waiting for the fullness of His victory to be completely manifest as it only will be when He returns. The kingdom of God has arrived decisively in Jesus, but not yet fully; and the kingdom of darkness has been defeated by Jesus, but is not yet eradicated. This chart can help us visualize our place in God's Story, as those who are living in what the Bible calls "the last days."

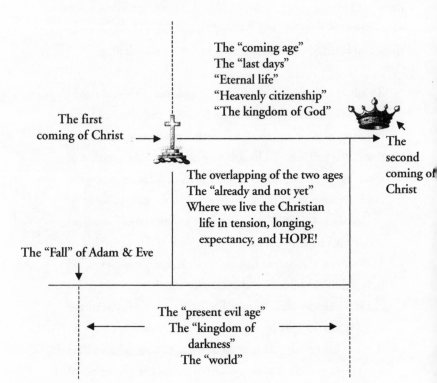

The "coming age"
The "last days"
"Eternal life"
"Heavenly citizenship"
"The kingdom of God"

The first
coming of Christ

The
second
coming of
Christ

The overlapping of the two ages
The "already and not yet"
Where we live the Christian
life in tension, longing,
expectancy, and HOPE!

The "Fall" of Adam & Eve

The "present evil age"
The "kingdom of
darkness"
The "world"

The second chart, created by Michael Green, portrays the overlapping of the two ages more effectively than the first. Let's be clear, however: we are not called just to *live* in the overlapping of the two ages, but to *serve* in this zone of "the already and not yet." As the Bride of Jesus, we are to see ourselves in the mop-up operation of D-Day as we await the glory of V-Day. We are not called to *bide our time*, but to *buy up the time*! Indeed, what on earth is Jesus doing that you need to be doing?

CHILDREN OF HOPE

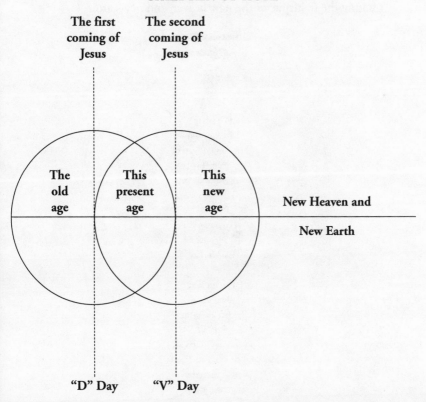

This final chart can help you visualize the intense conflict taking place for dominion over all things created by God. This is by no means an exhaustive list. But as you look at it, consider these questions: What evil on this earth are you meant to stand against? What darkness is your life spent on destroying? Are you only replicating middle-class living? Are you only decent? Which of the effects of the *Fall* are you enraged over and standing against? What on earth are you doing for Jesus' sake? How are you and your church family announcing Jesus' decisive victory over sin and death, and offering the firstfruits of the new heaven and new earth?

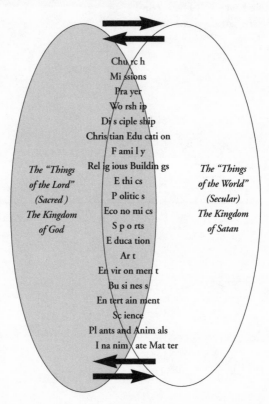

The "Things of the Lord" (Sacred) The Kingdom of God

Church
Missions
Prayer
Worship
Discipleship
Christian Education
Family
Religious Buildings
Ethics
Politics
Economics
Sports
Education
Art
Environment
Business
Entertainment
Science
Plants and Animals
Inanimate Matter

The "Things of the World" (Secular) The Kingdom of Satan

Two Opposing Dominions
Making Their Claim on "All Things"

Brokenness is manifest everywhere, as is the distinction between the already and not yet. The influence of two opposing kingdoms can be discerned by those who have wise hearts and trained sensibilities. Parents who place their children in Christian schools must not be naïve to think their kids are safe and protected. Spiritual warfare will be manifest there as intensely as in public schools. "Christian music," and all the trappings, business, and baggage involved, can be just as broken, dark, and unredeemed as "secular" mainstream music business and art.

Living Between the Already and Not Yet

There are two extremes we must avoid as we join Jesus in His commitment to make all things new. In which of these extremes are you most likely to show up? Consider journaling your thoughts and prayers as the issues raised in this chapter are calling you to faith and action.

We can underestimate the "already" dimension of Jesus' kingdom and live with little expectation of change occurring before He returns. This error is fueled by unbelief and leads to cultural disengagement, ingrown churches, fear-based discipleship, pragmatic spirituality, conspiracy theories, date-setting eschatology, and boring Christians.

On the other hand, we can disregard the "not yet" dimension of Jesus' kingdom and "claim" too much before He returns. This error is fueled by presumption and can be found in "word of faith churches," prosperity theology, "the health and wealth gospel," triumphalistic spirituality, and obnoxious Christians.

6 RESTORING BROKEN LIVES

"And I heard a loud voice from the throne saying, 'Behold, the dwelling place of God is with man. He will dwell with them, and they will be his people, and God Himself will be with them as their God. He will wipe away every tear from their eyes, and death shall be no more, neither shall there be mourning nor crying nor pain anymore, for the former things have passed away.' And He who was seated on the throne said, 'Behold, I am making all things new.' Also He said, 'Write this down, for these words are trustworthy and true.'"

—REVELATION 21:3–5

"I saw the face of Jesus in a little orphan girl
She was standing in the corner on the other side of the world
And I heard the voice of Jesus gently whisper to my heart,
'Didn't you say you wanted to find Me?
Well, here I am, here you are.
So, what now? What will you do now that you found Me?
What now?
What will you do with this treasure you have found?
I know I may not look like what you expected,
but remember this is right where I said I would be.
You've found Me . . . what now?'"

—SCC, "What Now?"

(STEVEN):

The doctors at Beijing Children's Hospital were taken aback—caring, but incredulous—as they surveyed Levi's ravaged, nearly lifeless form. "Why are you bothering with this baby? Wouldn't it be more merciful just to let him die? What kind of life do you think he's going to have . . . *if* he survives? Do you really think anyone would want to adopt such a child?"

Found abandoned in an open field—wrapped in a blanket stuffed with a Chinese bill worth little more than a U.S. dollar—this priceless life had been nearly burned to death. The doctors indicated there was a strong likelihood all of Levi's limbs would have to be amputated.

Are some people, things, and situations *too* broken to get involved with? Being woven into Levi's story has encouraged and convicted me that we *must not* give up so easily on messy situations and difficult people. Though all brokenness will be eliminated when Jesus returns, He is in the business of restoring broken things. And He is mightily at work today, accomplishing great things beyond our asking and imagining. Some of the very "messes" we concede as hopeless are the exact places God's mercies prove to be matchless.

Though the first few months of Levi's life were written with the ink of horrific pain, Jesus had more chapters to write with indelible grace. Two thousand years earlier, He told a parable comparing the kingdom of God to finding "treasure hidden in a field" (Matthew 13:44). Who could have imagined that finding Levi was meant as a powerful announcement that Jesus' redeeming kingdom has come to Langfang, Beijing, Boston, Franklin, and a whole lot of other places?

"Whatever it takes . . . do *whatever* it takes to help him. *This one matters."* My friend, Tim Baker, *pled* with the doctors who gave Levi only a 20 percent chance of survival. He promised that he and his wife, Pam, would adopt Levi if the lead physician at Beijing Children's Hospital would try to save his life. "I would be *proud* to have him as a son, and it will be a joy to see him graduate from high school and walk down the aisle on his wedding day." Tim's words were saturated with an alien love, and the skilled surgeon agreed to do her best to care for Levi.

The night before Levi's first surgery, Lisa Bentley, one of the Baker's colleagues, spent the evening beside Levi's incubator reading the Scriptures to him and soothing his little spirit through prayer and the cooing sounds emanating from her maternal instincts. As Levi gazed into her eyes, Lisa's heart nearly broke as she watched him try his best to suck his little burned thumb.

The morning came, and with it, new mercies. It was as though God had mobilized a multitude of angels, as the hospital staff in Beijing rallied around Levi with extraordinary interest and investment, both during surgery and afterward in his recovery. Their around-the-clock attention resulted in tremendous success. Levi not only survived, but when he was strong enough for the trip, he was flown to Boston, where the skilled staff at the Shriners Hospital performed additional surgeries—for free!

A COLONY OF HEAVEN

Getting to know the Bakers and others who work at Langfang has been a rare honor. It's also been sweet and dangerous: *sweet* because their hearts overflow with the tenderness and compassion of Jesus;

dangerous, because their lifestyle is a magnetic contagion of radical freedom and faith. It's hard *not* to want to follow them as they follow Jesus. They remind me of Scotty's spiritual dad—Jack Miller—who, before leaving us for heaven, would often visit church and invariably bring the convicting power of gospel joy, challenging us to "risk or rust." Jack's words still ring true: "God's grace is powerful enough to change anybody, anytime, anywhere!"

Children's Village, in Langfang, exists to care for special needs children like Levi, watching over these little lambs until they are placed in adoptive families, who will seek to love them with the restorative grace of Jesus. I think of the place, however, as a "colony of heaven" that, in the words of hymn writer Isaac Watts, "proves the wonders of his love."

I visited Children's Village for the first time in 2001, and my heart was both crushed and captured by a little girl now named Orly. Stone-faced and frighteningly detached, we could *not* get Orly to smile. It was from that encounter that I wrote, "What Now?," a song that laments the haunting face of brokenness in the face of a little orphan girl, yet invites us to find Jesus in her face and in that place—*and to respond.*

Enter Maria, the newest and final (though I've said that before) member of the Chapman family. Maria came into our hearts and home from that little colony of heaven in Langfang. When we first began the process of adopting Maria from Children's Village, we were informed she had a heart condition, and we counted it a joy to sign on for whatever it took to care for her. But either Jesus healed her or there had been a misdiagnosis, for when we brought Maria to Franklin, her heart was declared to be healthy and whole, for which we give God great praise.

Yet time and again, Jesus has proven to me just how generous He really is. And Easter 2004 will always stand out as one of the greatest measures of His generosity. I could hardly believe my eyes. Try to get this picture in your mind, make that your heart: Levi is *walking around*, giggling and smiling with other children on an Easter egg hunt. His basket is dangling across *one forearm*, while he picks up eggs with his surgically reconstructed *hand on his other arm*! And, as if a merry and mobile Levi is not enough to cause your heart to worship Jesus, add to that picture Orly, now vibrant and fully alive! She has now been adopted into one of the families who works there at Langfang, and Levi is in the process of being adopted as well. Doesn't it make all the sense in the world that this celebration of restoration would happen the very weekend we remember Jesus' resurrection and His complete victory over sin and death?!

Levi's story underscores the eternal value of *every single life*. There are *no* insignificant people, including *you*. We dare not look at anyone, including the person staring back at us in the mirror, and conclude, "Broken beyond repair." Jesus still leaves the ninety-nine for the one little lamb who is in desperate need. Jesus is coming after *you* . . . and He is reaching *through you* to *many* others. He is ready to prove the wonders of His love and multiply *more* colonies of heaven.

YOUR STORY OF PERSONAL RESTORATION

(Scotty:)

If you've never wondered what a completely sinless, healthy, and perfect *you* will be like, John's stunning proclamation in Revelation

21 is your personal invitation. The beloved disciple was given a sound bite and a sneak preview of the day when the wait of grace gives way to the weight of glory, and we will become *everything* God designed and Jesus died to make us. "Free at last, free at last . . . thank God, the Lord Almighty, we will be free at last!"

John's account begins with a thunderous, attention-riveting voice heralding from heaven—the much-awaited reunion between God and His people. The sheer volume and majesty of this decree fuels our anticipation for huge pageantry and bombast. Yet the first thing John describes is the hand of God delicately wiping away our tears and decisively wiping out all death, mourning, crying, and pain—forever! How fitting. How absolutely fitting for our loving God. He has always taken tears much more seriously than we have.

Unfortunately, many of us grew up despising, or at least being ashamed of, our tears. Some of us were told, "Big boys don't cry." Others were cruelly taunted with, "Don't be such a crybaby." Still others had what felt like the first layer of cheek skin rubbed off our faces when a parent or teacher wiped tears off our faces, as though they were getting rid of mustard or magic marker. The message was obvious: "Stand up straight. Be brave! Don't embarrass me with your weakness and whining."

But John's vision of the day when God will wipe away our tears conveys an altogether different message. The Greek text of Revelation 21:4 is better translated, "He will wipe out of their eyes every tear." The image is one of redemption, not resentment, of harvest, not harshness. For those who sow tears in this life are promised a harvest of everlasting joy in the next (Psalm 126:5). God's compassionate, tear-wiping hand will validate our wounds, and we will celebrate our wholeness on the day Jesus returns to make all things new.

Until then, our Father is mightily and mercifully at work to make each of His adopted children like His Son, Jesus. Though this process of restoration is painful at times, it hurts good—like the setting of a broken bone, or the cleansing of an infected wound, or the expelling of poisonous toxins. It's a healing journey, not with dry formulas, but with a dynamic flow.

A great place to enter this river of grace is through a song King David wrote celebrating God's original design for each of us.

O LORD, our Lord, how majestic is your name in all the earth! You have set your glory above the heavens. From the lips of children and infants you have ordained praise because of your enemies, to silence the foe and the avenger. When I consider your heavens, the work of your fingers, the moon and the stars, which you have set in place, what is man that you are mindful of him, the son of man that you care for him? You made him a little lower than the heavenly beings and crowned him with glory and honor. You made him ruler over the works of your hands; you put everything under his feet: all flocks and herds, and the beasts of the field, the birds of the air, and the fish of the sea, all that swim the paths of the seas (Psalm 8:1–8 NIV).

Reflecting on the glory of God's creation, David erupted into spontaneous praise. But praise gave way to astonishment as the implications of man's place in God's Story seized his worshiping heart. Through Psalm 8, this "man after God's own heart" shows us:

- We have *meaning*.
  We were *created in God's image* = Incomparable *design*

- We have *worth*.
  We are *crowned with God's glory* = Incalculable *dignity*

- We have *purpose*.
  We are *called into God's service* = Inestimable *destiny*

As God's image bearers, we were made to *revel in* and *reveal* His glory. However, because of sin, we "returned the favor" and remade God in *our* image, choosing to live for *our* glory rather than His. The only calling we care about is "calling the shots." How broken are we? Apart from God's intervention, we continually look to find our meaning, worth, and purpose *anywhere,* but in relationship with God. But God *has* intervened by sending Jesus into our broken world. He has come to restore the Father's image in us, and restore us to God's purposes. Therefore, we are broken to the degree we choose to live for *our* glory rather than God's glory.

Which Story and Whose Glory Define You?

A broken man is more preoccupied with his autobiography of personal reputation than with God's biography of cosmic restoration. This sabotage began when Satan first tempted Adam and Eve to put themselves at the center of their existence, in place of God. The restoration of an individual life, then, is an issue of *story* and *glory*. Though we are made to live in God's Story for His glory, a multitude of other plots (storylines or idol-myths) aggressively compete for our heart's affection and life direction.

The truth and beauty of the gospel expose these idol-myths as feeble substitutes and garish counterfeits. And the power of the gospel enables us to break free from their enslaving and destructive grasp. Indeed, as our deliverer and liberator, Jesus is freeing us for the great adventure of living as *characters in* and *carriers of* God's archetypal Story of all stories. It's like being taken from starring in your own self-produced, 8mm black-and-white home movies to playing one of the hobbits in the grand production of *The Return of the King*.

So how does Jesus bring us into a life of living as characters and carriers of God's Big Story? Steven and I share a common passion that helps to illustrate this process: fishing. There's a certain angling etiquette involved in sports-fishing—especially fly-fishing—that's known as "catch and release." This is an important discipline by which we fishermen enjoy *catching* various species of fish, and then *releasing* them uneaten and unharmed.

Fly-fishermen *revere the catch* and they *rejoice in the release* because, when it comes to fly-fishing, it's not primarily about "eats" but art. Fly-fishermen learn and employ all kinds of skills and techniques in the art of getting a trout to take their fly. But the real art is experienced when a sun-kissed Rainbow, or a Christmas-like Greenback Cutthroat, or a Rocky Mountain high-elevation, brightly-colored Speckled, or a golden-hued, fiery-red-dotted Brown trout is *briefly* held, delighted in, and rejoiced over before being released for the enjoyment of others. Jesus is the consummate fly-fisherman practicing "catch and release." And He is fishing the nations of the world.

CATCH—Becoming a *Character* in God's Story

This is your personal story—your account of being captured, loved, healed, and freed through the gospel. Jesus comes after you with all of the joy, delight, skill, patience, and persistence of a fly-fisherman. He will go to drastic and extreme measures to catch you. But His purpose is not to harm you. Rather, He will hold you, rejoice over you, delight in you, care for you, and free you for the benefit and joy of others.

RELEASE—Becoming a *Carrier* of God's Story

This is your missional story—your narrative of learning to live and love as a conduit of God's transforming grace. It's about finding your place in the Father's Big Story of redemption, restoration, and renewal. This is *you* becoming intentional and specific about a life of *worship service*, and giving Jesus your adoration, agenda, and accountability.

How Does Jesus Catch Us and Release Us?

The Book of Jonah provides invaluable insight into the ways of a broken man and the ways of our redeeming God. It also demonstrates how Jesus' work of renewal in the life of an individual believer connects with His larger work among the nations of the world.

Let's remember the basic story line of the Book of Jonah. God called Jonah to go to Nineveh, the capital of Assyria, and proclaim imminent judgment upon the people's sin and idolatries. Though the Assyrians were Israel's enemies, and Jonah would've *loved* to have seen the wrath of God fall on this barbaric people, the prophet was well aware that God had *bigger* plans for His creation than simply blessing Israel. But this was a part of the Father's Story, Jonah didn't "get" and wasn't about to glory in. Like many of us, his theology was better than his heart.

Jonah had a decision to make: could he squeeze God into his own little provincial story, or would he accept his place in the Father's pan-national Story? For Jonah, it was a "no-brainer" (literally), for he followed his prejudice rather than God's providence. Jonah plotted a course toward Tarshish, in the opposite direction of God's redeeming plot for Nineveh. The Book of Jonah reveals the different ways God "angled" to *catch* Jonah in order to *release* him into his bigger story of redemption.

CAUGHT BY THE STRATAGEMS OF GRACE

A good fly-fisherman comes prepared for *all* situations. He has a wide array of flies, fishing strategies, and types of casts to catch a treasure. Let's consider some of the different stratagems of grace God uses to "catch" and work in the lives of His sons and daughters, whom He treasures so much. How do we see Jesus coming after us in this Story?

The Promises of an Enormous Gospel

First and foremost, God uses the gospel of His grace to capture us. He lures us with the revelation of His merciful and generous heart for us, as proven through Jesus. Jonah knew this gospel, but unfortunately began to edit it. He took the DVD of the Bible we talked about earlier and made his own version of the good news. Consider the unreasonableness of the excuse Jonah gave for running away to Tarshish:

> "O LORD, is not this what I said when I was yet in my country? That is why I made haste to flee to Tarshish; for I knew that you are a gracious God and merciful, slow to anger and abounding in steadfast love, and relenting from disaster" (Jonah 4:2).

In essence, Jonah was saying, "I'm glad you're a gracious God, but I want you to be gracious on *my* terms." If there were a fifth chapter to the Book of Jonah, it wouldn't surprise me to discover that Jonah finally came to his senses. The revelation of God's outrageous promises for mankind has the power to humble us like nothing else. The more we expose ourselves to the study and consistent preaching of the gospel of God's grace, the more likely our idol structures will crumble and our foolish strivings for personal glory will be sabotaged.

Later in his ministry, Jesus spoke of "the sign of Jonah," even referring to himself as the "one greater than Jonah." Don't these affirmations suggest that Jonah finally realized that living by God's big, generous heart was much healthier than living by his raisin-sized, stingy heart?

The Persistence of Loving Pursuit

God proves Himself to be an all-weather fisherman. As Jonah's story unfolds, we see God's unrelenting commitment to have His beloved son and His glory revealed among the nations, including Nineveh. Early in Jonah's sea-bound flight to Tarshish, God sent a wind and a storm upon the sea—the first indication to the prophet that he could run, but not *outrun* the God of all grace. The remainder of the story demonstrates the pursuing heart of God.

What zephyrs of mercy and waves of attention-getting compassion has God used in your past? Have you noticed any storm clouds gathering recently? Is this a season in which the hound of heaven may be hounding you for your good? None of us should be presumptuous about God's goodness, but neither should we be naïve about His resolve to accomplish His work in our lives. It's important to notice that the harder Jonah ran from God, the more God "upped the ante" on the severity of His mercy. Far better to pay attention to waves and storms than be swallowed by the "Shamu"!

The Providence of Annoying Circumstances

God's sovereign "appointments" come in many forms. In addition to the wind and storm in the Book of Jonah, God "appointed a great fish to swallow up Jonah" (1:17); and a plant, a worm, and a scorching east wind to reach the heart of His wayward son (4:6–8).

None of us should try to make a tit-for-tat correlation between every annoyance and some specific message from God. But the Book of Jonah certainly teaches us that maintaining a teachable, convictable heart is a wise way to live. Don't simply categorize difficult circumstances to "life in a fallen world" or the "discouraging tactics of the devil."

The Presence of Unsuspecting People

As the storm grew more and more violent, pagan seamen and the ship's captain became the voice of God in Jonah's story. Consider the questions they asked God's rebellious son: "How can you sleep? Who is responsible for making all this trouble for us? What is your job? Where do you come from? What is your country? From what people are you? What have you done?"

God has a history of using a wide array of people—even donkeys—to get the attention of His sons and daughters. This doesn't mean it's wise to seek important counsel from nonbelievers. Rather, it highlights that God may use a highway patrolman, an AA group, a high-school principle, an IRS representative, an ER surgeon, an angry neighbor, an AIDS victim, a co-worker—he can use *anyone* to get your attention. Are you paying attention?

The Prodding of Challenging Questions

"Have you any right to be angry?" "Do you have a right to be angry about the [vine]?" "Should I not be concerned about that great city?" (Jonah 4:4, 9, 11 NIV). God doesn't usually ask many "yes" or "no" questions, for He never asks *any* question in search of information. What does He not know? Rather, He asked Jonah questions for the same reason He asks you and me questions: to expose *our* hearts to *His* heart.

Take a good look at the questions God presented Jonah. How would you answer the same questions? Are there other specific questions or particular lines of questioning that Jesus seems to be placing before you in this season of life? What are they?

The Pain of Disruptive Grace

Just how determined is God to make us *characters in* and *carriers of* the only story worth living in and dying for? How would you like to spend three days sloshing around in the stomach acids of a large salt-water creature? And then be deposited on the beach through projectile vomiting? I agree, it's a pretty disgusting thought—but not as disgusting as the choice Jonah made to live for his own glory.

The only time we see Jonah manifesting "gospel sanity" is when he experienced the terribly uncomfortable circumstance of God's disruptive grace. Take a close look at the words of a sane man: "Those who cling to worthless idols forfeit the grace that could be theirs. . . . Salvation comes from the LORD" (2:8–9 NIV).

In this one brief moment, Jonah "got it." He understood that God alone is worthy of our worship service. We are crazy to put *anything* in His place, for it only leads to a forfeiture of His grace. The lights may have come on as Jonah floated in the belly of a fish, but not in the recesses of Jonah's heart. Though he did go to Nineveh, Jonah went with resentment, and not with the joy of being resent as a humbled participant in God's great love affair with the nations of sinful men.

Take a moment and reflect. When have you encountered God's disruptive grace? Perhaps you have never considered looking at painful circumstances as a means of coming to "gospel sanity." I'll emphasize this point again: there is no merit or warrant in looking for a tit-for-tat correlation between specific things you have done and hard providences you have experienced. That tends to lead to "the paralysis of analysis," and, usually, to self-pity and self-righteousness.

Just start taking my grandmother's advice seriously: "Jesus loves you just the way you are, but too much to leave you the way you are." Jesus has come to set captives free, not just to hold their hand during prison visits.

What does it mean to "forfeit grace"?

To forfeit grace does not mean we lose our *acceptance with God.* Rather, we rob our hearts of *rich fellowship with God.* When we forfeit the grace that could be ours, we rob others as well.

Who else did Jonah rob?

Jonah robbed sailors and a sea captain of his knowledge of the one true God. He robbed his family of the gift of watching a husband, dad, son, and sibling wrestle with the will of God. He robbed his closest friends and fellow believers of the joy and pain of struggling and growing together in community. He robbed the Ninevites of the beauty of enemies being reconciled.

But, most tragically, Jonah robbed God of His glory.

How do we forfeit grace?

We forfeit grace by choosing to be our own savior. Jonah paid his own fare to Tarshish. We forfeit grace by clinging to "worthless idols." Typically, idolatry is born out of a commitment to live in our story for our glory. We choose an idol we believe will give us meaning and worth. For example, Jonah chose to idolize nationalism to fulfill His story and give Him glory. "Life will only have meaning if God makes my nation superior to all other nations." How powerful is idol worship? Jonah preferred death over the thought of being in relationship with Ninevites. Idolatry is destructive fanaticism.

IDOL-MYTHS WE CHOOSE TO FULFILL OUR STORIES AND GIVE US GLORY

Tim Keller, senior pastor of Redeemer Presbyterian Church in Manhattan, has composed a helpful list identifying many of the prevailing idols we tend to worship in our contemporary culture. I give him many thanks and deep appreciation for this convicting profile.

- Power idolatry: "Life only has meaning/I only have worth if . . . I have power and influence over others."

- Approval idolatry: "Life only has meaning/I only have worth if . . . I am loved and respected by _____."

- Comfort idolatry: "Life only has meaning/I only have worth if . . . I have (this kind) of pleasure experience, a particular quality of life."

- Image idolatry: "Life only has meaning/I only have worth if . . . I have a particular kind of look or body image."

- Control idolatry: "Life only has meaning/I only have worth if . . . I am able to get mastery over my life in the area of _____."

- Helping idolatry: "Life only has meaning/I only have worth if . . . people are dependent on me and need me."

- Dependence idolatry: "Life only has meaning/I only have worth if . . . someone is there to protect me and keep me safe."

- Independence idolatry: "Life only has meaning/I only have worth if . . . I am completely free from obligations or responsibilities to take care of someone."

- Work idolatry: "Life only has meaning/I only have worth if . . . I am highly productive getting a lot done."

- Achievement idolatry: "Life only has meaning/I only have worth if . . . I am being recognized for my accomplishments or if I am excelling in my career."

- Materialism idolatry: "Life only has meaning/I only have worth if . . . I have a certain level of wealth, financial freedom, and nice possessions.

- Religion idolatry: "Life only has meaning/I only have worth if . . . I am adhering to my religion's moral codes and am accomplished in its activities."

- Individual person idolatry: "Life only has meaning/I only have worth if . . . this one person in my life is happy (especially with me)."

- Irreligion idolatry: "Life only has meaning/I only have worth if . . . I feel I am totally independent of organized religion and with a self-made morality."

- Racial/cultural idolatry: "Life only has meaning/I only have worth if . . . my race and culture is ascendant and recognized as superior."

- Inner-ring idolatry: "Life only has meaning/I only have worth if . . . a particular social group, professional group, or other group lets me in."

- Family idolatry: "Life only has meaning/I only have worth if . . . my children and/or my parents are happy (especially with me)."

- Relationship idolatry: "Life only has meaning/I only have worth if . . . Mr. or Ms. Right is in love with me."

- Suffering idolatry: "Life only has meaning/I only have worth if . . . I am hurting or in a problem. Only then do I feel noble or worthy of love or am able to deal with guilt."

- Ideology idolatry: "Life only has meaning/I only have worth if . . . my political or social cause or party is making progress and ascending in influence or power.[1]

DEFYING THE ODDS

As this list indicates, idols are all around us on a daily basis. Couple this with our innate nature to serve anything but God, and it makes for a scene as deprived as Ninevah. The key is falling on the grace of God to help us cast aside all idols. Like Shadrach, Meshach, and Abednego, we can stand in the midst of an idol-worshiping culture and refuse to bow to anything but the one true God (Daniel 3:16–18).

How did these three young men stand up against such life-or-death odds? God had restored them. He had proven His faithfulness to them again and again, just as He proved His faithfulness to both Jonah and all of Ninevah. The Father's desire isn't to destroy but to restore. He *wanted* to save Ninevah from self-destruction simply because that is His loving and gracious heart. He *wants* to save you from whatever idols you tend to put up, not because He can't topple them but because He wants your untarnished love and devotion. Like a wise fisherman, God pursues you as His prize catch—waiting to be caught, yes; but even greater, waiting to be released into a future of complete hope and restoration.

7 RESTORING BROKEN RELATIONSHIPS

"And I heard a loud voice from the throne saying, 'Behold, the dwelling place of God is with man. He will dwell with them, and they will be his people, and God himself will be with them as their God. He will wipe away every tear from their eyes.'"

—REVELATION 21:3-4

"A day is coming that won't fade to night
There'll be no more hatred to endure, no wars to fight
There'll be no orphans, no prisoners or slaves
And all the tears of death and pain will be washed away
This day is coming ... it's surely coming
Jesus, You're coming"

— SCC, "Coming Attractions"

(STEVEN):

Steven Curtis, please meet my dear friend, Mincaye—or as my children call him, *Mamae*, grandfather—the man who speared my father to death." It's a good thing I wasn't drinking a glass of chocolate milk while my friend Steve Saint was making this introduction; I would have either spewed Hershey's chocolate syrup on the elderly Waodani tribesman, or I would have choked in trying to swallow

117

the combination of these conflicting images. *"My dear friend, grand-father to my children . . . the man who speared my father to death."*

There are some things that just *don't* belong together. Canned asparagus doesn't belong on top of a bowl of peppermint ice cream. You'll never catch Scotty in a Duke sweatshirt. Emeril isn't going to ask me to join the Food Channel as his French pastry chef. And, *most certainly*, a son would *never* call his father's murderer "dear friend," nor would his children *ever* call the one who killed their biological grandfather *"Mamae"* . . . because some things just *don't* belong together. Or so I thought.

The gospel of God's grace challenges and changes *everything*. God has written us into an unprecedented and revolutionary story of *reconciliation*, in which hostilities are destroyed and enemies become friends—where, one day, wolves and lambs will lie down together, and lions and calves will eat straw side by side (Isaiah 11).

There is nothing in John's vision of life in the new heaven and new earth that causes me more joy than the promise of living forever in healed and perfected relationships. For nothing confirms the brokenness of God's world and people more than the fractured, clumsy, ugly, and destructive ways we relate to one another.

I know this to be true first hand. When Mary Beth and I walked through the portals of the front door with "Care for Orphans" written over it in large letters, we stepped into a world *filled* with stories revealing the power of sin and death to divide, devastate, and destroy families. I've witnessed this destructive power up-close through the painful reality of my parent's divorce, and I see it making a bid for marriages everywhere I look—including in the mirror.

Whether I'm in China (seeing the painful evidence of how communism has ravaged the relational structure of hundreds of millions of people), or walking down Main Street of Franklin, (my small community in which the vestiges of racism, elitism, and cultural pride still linger from the Civil War), I find myself *increasingly* longing for the tear-wiping hand of God to reach into our world to heal broken relationships and bring us into our promised eternity of loving perfectly forever.

What's Impossible With Man . . .

Whenever I am tempted to question Jesus' ability to do the impossible or find myself doubting that He is, indeed, actively making all things new, I just glance at the bookshelf where I keep a short stack of books God has used to change my life. None of those books has had a greater impact on my confidence in the power of the gospel than my old, worn copy of Elisabeth Elliot's *Through Gates of Splendor*. It's the powerful and inspiring story of five men who followed God's call to take the gospel to the remote jungles of Ecuador, only to meet a tragic end—tragic in the eyes of the world, but the triumph God brought about in the years that followed is nothing less than miraculous. Little did I know, as I was engrossed in the intriguing story, how my life would intersect with this amazing story of reconciliation that happened in a remote corner of the world.

Through Gates of Splendor tells the story of four college friends—Jim Elliot, Pete Fleming, Roger Youderian, and Ed McCully—who took their wives and children deep into the jungles of South America in 1955. They teamed up with Nate Saint, a pilot with

Mission Aviation Fellowship (MAF) in Ecuador. Nate was there with his wife, Marj, to serve the needs of missionaries who required transportation in and out of the dense rainforest landscape. The book details the call on the lives of these five men to reach a savage tribe known as the Auca. Little was known about the tribe, except that they were extremely violent. Only years before, members of the tribe had killed a group of oil company workers who made the fatal error of traveling into the land of the Auca.

One of the main concerns for the missionaries was the inter-tribal warfare taking place. Offenses between tribes were usually dealt with by night raids, during which the offender and his entire family would be killed by spear or machete. The Auca believed that if you left any member of the offender's family alive, that person would be obligated to return and exact vengeance against the attacker's family. It was an endless cycle of violence that threatened the very survival of the Auca.

As these five missionaries learned of these events in the jungles so far away, John's vision of the tear-wiping God gathering His people from every nation—healing them and making them one family—enflamed their hearts. They had learned that the Ecuadorian government was considering plans to move against the tribe because of the relentless killing. God placed a burden in their hearts to take the gospel of His grace and literally save the Aucas from extinction.

What faith these men had to leave the comforts of life in the U.S. and travel to an uncharted region of the world where the way of life in the jungle was one dominated by violence. Nate had done extensive flights over the land of the Auca. He came up with a plan to make contact with the Auca by dropping gifts from the plane.

Nate created an ingenious device that allowed him to lower gifts in a bucket while his small plane hovered overhead and flew in a circle. They would lower gifts down into the villages where the Auca were living.

An amazing thing began to happen. After a season of receiving gifts from the missionaries, the Auca tribesmen began giving gifts *to the missionaries*, placing the items in the bucket that would be raised back up to the plane. That was the sign the men were hoping for. Since they had made a friendly contact, the men believed it was time to meet the Auca face-to-face.

Nate carefully landed the little plane on the beach near the village. Imagine how his heart raced, along with the others, when within a few days, a man and two women emerged from the jungle to meet him. It was a glorious answer to prayer—a friendly encounter with these people they had heard so much about. The amazing encounter was captured on film, and it's fascinating to view the events of that day in the jungle. The missionaries thanked God for His gift of that meeting and hoped it would develop into a friendship that would allow them to share the message of the gospel and God's love for them.

Jim Elliot, Pete Fleming, Roger Youderian, Ed McCully, and Nate Saint set up camp and named their little beach Palm Beach. They talked and prayed and waited for the natives to return. Three days passed and no sign of life. Then, suddenly, a group of men emerged from the jungle with weapons of death. All five missionaries were killed with machetes and spears.

Although the missionaries had a gun with them, they made a pact not to use the weapon to defend themselves. They would only use the gun to try to scare the tribesmen, if such a move was necessary to explain their reason for coming. But they never got that chance. Their lifeless bodies were scattered on the sand, and the Auca retreated into the jungle.

THE ULTIMATE REDEMPTION

"Five Missionaries Martyred in the Jungles of Ecuador" was the headline flashed around the world. *Life* magazine ran an extensive story including the gruesome photos. Every newspaper in the U.S. covered the story, and many questioned why five gifted men would sacrifice their lives to try to reach a savage people. But that was not the end of the story.

What happened next is nothing short of amazing. As they mourned the loss of their husbands, the widows thought, *What do we do now that our husbands have been killed? Do we go back home? Go back to the U.S. and consider this a failed mission?* Elisabeth Elliot sensed God speaking to her heart, calling her to continue the work begun by her husband and the other missionaries—to go back to the very tribe that had taken the life of her husband. And so she went. Joining her was Nate Saint's sister, Rachel, who was a Wycliffe Bible translator.

As Rachel, Elisabeth, and the Elliots' young daughter, Valerie, went to live with the tribe, they took with them a powerful message of love and forgiveness. They slowly began to learn to communicate that they had come as the wife and sister of the men whom the tribesmen had killed. They explained that their kin had come in peace, not to harm them, but to help them.

The Auca were suspicious of Elisabeth and Rachel. In the beginning of their time in the jungle, the women were subject to constant death threats. Members of the tribe assumed they had returned to avenge the murder of their loved ones. In time, they would come to know it was the love of God that drew them back.

How would Rachel and Elisabeth communicate with the Auca? How would they learn their language? God answered this prayer, as He often does, through the life of one of His broken children. Her name was Dayuma. As a young child, she had lost her entire family in a tribal raid. She escaped and had lived far away for many years. Dayuma returned with Elisabeth and Rachel and helped them communicate with the Aucas.

Slowly, God began to work in that tribe, leading to the glorious day when many of the same men who killed those missionaries became believers in Jesus! Rachel Saint dedicated her life to the Auca people and lived among them for more than three decades.

This amazing account of the reconciling power of the gospel first gripped my heart about thirty-seven miles up in our atmosphere, as I was flying to a concert date. With tears filling my eyes, I felt an unusually strong connection to this story. What began as a fanciful dream—that I would actually visit the village in Ecuador where this story took place—turned into a surprise connection with one of the sons of the martyred missionaries.

An Internet search led me to the name "Steve Saint," the son of Nate Saint, the team pilot who was murdered when Steve was just five. I found some articles Steve had written about the ongoing work with the Waodani tribe (Auca are now called Waodani). He founded a missions outreach ministry called I-TEC (Indigenous

Technology Education) that was originally birthed to work with the Waodani tribe and other indigenous people groups.

I found the number for I-TEC and called the office in Florida with the hope of speaking to Steve. Though he wasn't in, it wasn't long before Steve left a message on my cell phone. When I heard his voice you would have thought Billy Graham had called me. I was literally shaking, realizing I was about to make a personal connection with this story that had been deeply planted in my heart.

We soon began a dialog that developed into a friendship. I shared with Steve that I had written some songs about the story of his father and the others that would be included on my next album. I was hoping for the opportunity to meet him, play him the songs, and share how I was being influenced by the story of the miracle in the jungle.

When we eventually got together, Steve provided more details about what happened that fateful day in 1956. There were six Auca men and some women who returned to the beach where the missionaries had set up camp. The women were sent as a decoy to wade out into the water toward the missionaries. As the five Americans saw the natives approaching, they thought they were coming back for a friendly encounter, so they waded out into the water to meet them. As they entered the water, they were ambushed from behind. One of the men who did the killing was Mincaye.

"Mincaye became a Christian several years ago," Steve told me. "My aunt Rachel was able to lead him to Christ, and he is now one of the greatest leaders of the Waodani church. He's an elder and evangelist and has become such a dear friend to me."

After his father was killed, Steve moved away from the jungle with his mother to Ecuador's capitol city of Quito. He returned in the summers to visit his aunt Rachel, who was living with the Waodani tribe. Little Stevie loved his time in the jungle. The men of the tribe welcomed him as one of their own sons, teaching him the ways of the jungle. Young Steve learned how to hunt for food with a blowgun and how to spear fish in the shimmering streams.

After living thirty-four years with the Waodoni people, Aunt Rachel went to be with the Lord. The entire tribe had come to love this beloved sister in Christ, who they affectionately called "Star"—*Nemo,* in their language. When Steve returned to the jungle with his four children to bury his dear aunt, the tribe made a surprising request: "Would you now come and live with us because Nemo is gone?"

Steve was moved by the invitation, but he explained that he had a business to run and a family to provide for. "I just can't come and live in the jungle," he told them. But God began to speak to Steve and his wife, Ginny, and they felt His call to return to live with the Waodoni people. For a year and a half, Steve and Ginny and their two youngest children lived in the jungle. Steve told me that, during that time, his children began to call Mincaye "*Mamae,*" the tribal word for grandfather. It's a term of great respect given to elder men in the tribe.

CONNECTING TO THE STORY

"Would you like to meet Mincaye?" Steve's question took me by surprise.

"Are you kidding?" I asked. "That would be incredible. I'd love to!"

Steve told me that Mincaye was coming to visit him in Florida. He also told me more about the way the Lord had worked in the lives of the Waodoni since his father and the others had been killed. When Elisabeth Elliot and Rachel Saint arrived, they began to share the gospel with the Aucas, telling them, "God doesn't want you to kill one another. There's a God who created you, and He loves you very much." As they continued to speak of God's love, a few of the people in the tribe became Christians, followed by an outright miracle: the intertribal killing stopped almost immediately! As the truth of the gospel moved through the tribe, the swords were quite literally turned into plowshares.

Over the years, Mincaye would occasionally come to spend time with Steve and his family. He would go with Steve to speak at mission conferences and even appeared a few times at Billy Graham evangelistic gatherings. Since Mincaye spoke no English, Steve would translate while the elder statesman of the Waodoni shared the story of how God transformed his life.

I'll never forget the day Steve and Mincaye came to my home. There before me were two men with an amazing story of lives weaved together by God's grace. Mincaye brought a blowgun made by his tribe to give to my children. His smile was infectious. His coal black hair and chiseled face set off his engaging and twinkling eyes. With Steve translating, Mincaye began to share his story with me in a beautiful language I had never heard, which was called Wao-Tededo. But then I got another surprise: Mincaye blessed me with a song from his tribe called "The Heaven Creation Song." I was able to record his singing in my studio and included the beautiful sounds on the song, "No Greater Love," on my album *Declaration*.

After Mincaye finished his song, I sang a song back to him. Although he couldn't understand the words, he seemed to really enjoy the music. As our time together unfolded, Mincaye, speaking through Steve, asked me a startling question. "I have come to you. Will you now come to visit my village? Will you come to my home and sing for my people?"

I knew that I had to go. This had been a desire of my heart, and now this dream of going to the place in the jungle—with so much history—looked like it would be coming true. Over the next several months, I made two trips to the jungle of Ecuador. On one of the trips, I was even able to take my two sons, Caleb and Will Franklin.

It's hard to explain what it was like to go and visit that place and to actually feel the sand beneath my feet in the same area where those five servants of the Lord lost their lives. I stood there beside Mincaye, next to this godly man who had been so tenderized by the gospel and restored by its power.

At one point, he had been filled with so much rage and hatred that he could take his spear and kill another person who had simply come to rescue his soul. Now he stood beside me praying an incredible prayer, thanking God for His mercy and for His grace. My heart was overflowing with gratitude for the privilege of the moment God allowed me to experience.

SHARING THE STORY

Standing there on the beach with Mincaye, I had a crazy idea. *What if I could share this with people every night on stage? What if people could experience this powerful story every night in one of my concert tours?*

While I was in Ecuador, Steve introduced me to two other men who were part of the attack party on the beach, Kimo and Dewey (sic). These two Waodani men had also become Christians and, along with Mincaye, were some of the godliest, most gentle men I've ever met. The power of the gospel had changed their lives, and they had become leaders in the Waodoni church.

When I returned home, I asked Steve if Mincaye would consider coming and being a part of some of my concerts. I never dreamed that he would be able to do the whole tour with us. Every night, I shared Steve and Mincaye's story through a short video and with music we performed live. Night after night, at the end of the dramatic presentation, I said, "You've heard the story. You saw the little five-year-old boy in those pictures who lost his father that day. Now I'd like to introduce you to that little boy, who is now a man, named Steve Saint." When he walked onstage, you could hear people gasp—it was a powerful moment every night. The audiences couldn't believe that this man was here.

I would sing one of the songs that was inspired by Steve Saint's story, called "God Is God."

God is God and I am not
I only see a part of the picture He is painting
God is God and I am man
So I'll never understand it all
Only God is God

After I finished singing the song each night, Steve would tell a deeply personal story that showed me more about God renewing and restoring broken things than any story I've ever heard.

Mincaye had come to visit Steve and his family in Florida. They had been asked to come and speak at a Billy Graham missions conference. Steve's family was always happy when Mincaye came into their home. He was dearly loved and truly was a part of the family. It was as if a grandfather was coming to visit. During this particular visit, Steve's only daughter, Stephanie, had come home from a missions trip. The twenty-year-old had spent about a year with a music mission team, and her homecoming was a great celebration.

Steve was so excited to have his daughter home. Judging by the way Steve told this story, Stephanie was obviously a daddy's girl. Since she had returned home on her birthday, the family was throwing a wonderful party for her.

But that evening, Stephanie began to feel sick and developed a tremendous headache that put her in bed early. Steve and his wife, Ginny, were at her bedside praying earnestly that their precious daughter would get relief from the pounding in her head. They did their best to comfort her, but Stephanie's headache got worse and worse.

That night, Stephanie seemed to fall unconscious. They quickly rushed her to the hospital and knew something extremely bad was happening. But the doctors' attempts to revive her didn't work. She had suffered a massive brain aneurysm and had literally died in her father's arms.

When Mincaye walked in and saw all the sophisticated medical equipment and needles connected to Stephanie, he became agitated and almost enraged. Being a tribal warrior, he couldn't understand what was going on. "Who is doing this to Stephanie?" he asked. "Who is doing this to my precious granddaughter?" Steve explained to Mincaye, "No man is doing this to her. This is her body; something is happening inside her body."

Mincaye had an immediate change of expression. It was as if a light had gone off in his mind, and he said, "I see this now. I understand. God is doing this. God is taking Stephanie to His place, to heaven—to His place to live with Him there. This is not a tragedy. This is a good thing. God is taking her to heaven."

And then something amazing happened. Mincaye began to speak with supernatural power to the doctors and nurses in the emergency room. He was filled with understanding, filled with the power of God's Spirit as he spoke in his beautiful language: "Do you see this, people? Do you understand that Stephanie is going to God's place? She is going to heaven. She is going to be with God. Are you going to be with God? All of us will leave this earth. Are you ready? Will you be in God's place with us? And will you go with us? I am an old man. I will go soon to God's place too. Will you go? Are you ready to go?"

Steve shared that story every night from stage and then would say the words I never tired of hearing: "So would you please welcome to the stage Grandfather Mincaye." And Mincaye would walk out on stage every night to the amazement of the crowd. I still get tears in my eyes thinking about how incredible that moment was every time, and how God had allowed me to be a part of this unfolding of the gospel.

I also observed daily how Steve served Mincaye. He was really like a child in our culture, so completely out of his element. Even little things, like learning how to turn sink faucets on, were new experiences for him. Steve helped him get cleaned up and ready for the concert each night. To see him loving the man who killed his father was a living testimony of God making all things new.

And Mincaye loved his time on stage. Here was a seventy- or eighty-year-old man (nobody really knows how old he is for sure, because there is no birth certificate), jumping up and down, his little face beaming, his heart filled with joy in anticipation of sharing his story. "I acted badly, badly, badly," he would tell the audience, "and then they brought me God's carvings." Every eye was fixed on this commanding presence as he continued. "God, taking His Holy Spirit, opened my eyes to understand that this was the good Word that they were speaking to me. I began to see that my heart was black."

Washing My Heart

Mincaye would explain the gospel the same way, night after night. As he shared his testimony, he would say, "God, taking the blood of Jesus, and, like us, would wash clothes with soap, He began to wash my heart. And He made my heart clean."

As I heard Mincaye share his story, I thought, *God, that's my story. I'm no different than this man. Your Word makes it so clear that all of us are murderers in our hearts if we've ever had a hateful thought toward another person. God, this is my story, this is how broken I was, but You have made me whole. You have made Mincaye whole.*

When a reporter from *USA Today* came to cover the tour and the story of Steve and Mincaye, he found the true story hard to believe. He told Steve, "You know, I can almost understand how you could forgive this man, maybe, or at least be able to tolerate that he was acting in ignorance and didn't understand what he was doing. But to *love* this man, to love him as your own father, to embrace him that way, that's almost more than I can comprehend." That is, I believe, just the testimony of what God does when He restores broken things. Things that are broken beyond our comprehension, and beyond repair, can be made new by the power of the gospel.

Steve Saint is one of my greatest mentors. I am so thankful for the time we've been able to spend together. As he told people each night about losing his father when he was a little boy, and then losing his own daughter, Steve would share how many would comment on what a hard life he had experienced. And despite his personal tragedies and trials, he would smile and say, "I have come to learn that God *never* wastes a hurt."

LIVING AS RESTORERS OF BROKEN RELATIONSHIPS

The story of Steve and Mincaye is a truly remarkable testimony of God's power to restore relationships. Whereas the world's eye-for-an-eye system would have had Steve seeking revenge for his father's death, God's system is one of love and redemption, and it led to a powerful relationship between the unlikeliest of friends. As representatives of the Prince of Peace, each of us is called to bring the restorative grace of Jesus into our broken relational world and into every one of our relationships. While we may not all face the tragic circumstances of Steve's life, we are to respond with the same love he showed.

The apostle Paul summarized this calling in one succinct verse: "If possible, so far as it depends on you, live peaceably with all" (Romans 12:18). To live "peaceably" means that we seek to bring the "shalom," or the peace of God, into relationships. A "shalom-ed" relationship is one in which there is order—that is, *alignment, health, integration, celebration*—just the way God designed relationships to be. Our calling is to bring some of the peace, or "order," of the future cosmos—the new heaven and new earth—into the present chaos.

Notice the two important qualifications Paul makes. First, he says to live peaceably with all, *so far as it depends on you*. Each of us must make the initiative in peacemaking and take responsibility for *ourselves* in all of our relationships. We are to be peacemakers "as unto the Lord," not making our obedience contingent on anyone's response.

Practically speaking, there are a few steps you can take to offer Jesus the worship service of peacemaking. Above all, keep your relationship with Jesus "hot," current, and vital, for we are to love one another as Jesus loves us (John 13:34). The indicatives of the gospel lead to the imperatives of love. We will seek to make peace in our world to the extent that we stay alive to the peace Jesus has made with us.

Seek healing and freedom in response to your past relational wounds. Much peacemaking requires declaring war—confronting the evil that brought harm to your soul and getting equipped to care for others who have been similarly sinned against and harmed. For many of us, the most important work of restoration in which we will be involved will flow out of an abusive past.

Hate whatever threatens peace among the brethren, and *cling* to whatever promotes restoration. Nothing threatens peace more than a foolish use of the tongue, and nothing promotes restoration more than its wise use. "Naming the animals" was one of the awesome callings God gave Adam in the Garden. But calling people "names," or cursing those made in the image of God, is the ultimate perversion of this sacred calling. Remember the following when bringing about peace with the words you say:

Hate gossip—both listening to it and dishing it out—like you hate cancer.

Do not use your tongue to "repeat" matters—i.e., to confess someone else's sin.

Do not use your tongue to conjecture out loud about a situation when your information is incomplete.

Do not use your tongue to editorialize on a situation or to label a person.

Use your tongue to pray with those with whom you are most likely to gossip.

Nothing is more critical to restoring broken relationships than learning how to receive and extend forgiveness. Peacemakers learn to forgive, as the Lord has forgiven us.

Unforgiveness is the poison we drink while hoping others will die.

To forgive is to violate all the rules for keeping score.

We are commanded to forgive, but we can never demand forgiveness from anyone.

Forgiving is not forgetting or ignoring an offense.

Forgiving is not excusing, justifying, or pardoning an offense.

Forgiving is not smothering a conflict.

Forgiving is not tolerating what should not be tolerated.

Forgiving does not always result in reconciliation.

Forgiving does not mean you stop hurting.

Forgiving is refusing to punish.

Forgiving is a commitment not to repeat or discuss the matter with others.

Forgiving is a radical commitment to uproot any residual bitterness.

Forgiving is a choice to be merciful as God your Father has been merciful with you.

These are all ways we can either establish peace or avoid disrupting it. But Paul also instructs us to live peaceably with all, *if possible*. There are circumstances that qualify the extent to which we may be able to experience peacemaking and restoration in various relationships.

There may be unwillingness from the other party(ies) to engage in restoration. In these situations, the peacemaker must settle for the "peace" that he has done everything within his power to work for reconciliation and restoration.

Some relationships may be *too* broken. Some relationships will require heaven to heal. Certain stories of abuse, infidelities, evil, and "monsters" require a miracle. But let us not forget Steve's story. Who would have ever thought a son could ever call the man who murdered his father a *precious friend*?

The timing for restoration may not be right. Time, in and of itself, heals nothing, but some relationships require time, plus much grace from God. The restoration between Joseph and his brothers is a prime example (Genesis 49–50).

From now on, therefore, we regard no one according to the flesh. Even though we once regarded Christ according to the flesh, we regard him thus no longer. Therefore, if anyone is in Christ, he is a new creation. The old has passed away; behold, the new has come. All this is from God, who through Christ reconciled us to himself and gave us the ministry of reconciliation; (that is, in Christ God was reconciling) the world to himself, not counting their trespasses against them, and entrusting to us the message of reconciliation (2 Corinthians 5:16–19).

8 RESTORING BROKEN WORSHIP

"I did not see a temple in the city, because the Lord God Almighty and the Lamb are its temple. The city does not need the sun or the moon to shine on it, for the glory of God gives it light, and the Lamb is its lamp."
—REVELATION 21:22–23 NIV

"What can I do, how can I live
To show my world the treasure of Jesus?
What will it take, what could I give
So they can know the treasure He is?"
—SCC, "Treasure of Jesus"

(STEVEN):

Group hug, group hug!" It was a typical Monday morning, and as the resident "Tigger" in our family (as my clan has labeled me), I was wearing my cheerleader hat and using my shepherd's crook to get our three oldest children off to school. Peering through slits where there should be eyes, the boys offered little more than a grunt-like groan in response to my hearty "Good morning!"

Emily appeared particularly tired, and she wasn't in any mood for her brothers' half-speed, half-hearted movements in the direction of her Beetle. On most days, Emily is as non-temperamental as teenagers come. But that morning, her frustration was about to boil over with her brothers. Being the oldest, she inherited the joy of driving the three of them to school every day. "We're going to be late! You guys hurry up!"

It proved to be one of those important moments when, as a dad, I got a glimpse of my own heart as I watched my daughter wrestle with the intrusive, irritating, and exasperating three or four hours we call "Monday morning"—a weekly event that has taken on cliché status in our culture. The problem for believers is that Monday morning immediately follows Sunday. We mark Sundays as "the Lord's Day," setting it aside to begin a new week by loving and worshiping God together as the people of God. Yet, given our spiritual realignment on Sundays, you'd think that "Monday morning" wouldn't show up *at least* till about Wednesday afternoon or at breakfast on Thursday!

Emily's brief jaunt from the adoration of Sunday to the agitation of Monday was a visible parable of how sin has broken God's worship, and of just how broken *we are* as his worshipers. Let me hasten to say, I don't know *anyone* who loves to worship God more than Emily. I love to watch my daughter give herself so fully and freely to the worship of Jesus. And that's what made this particular Monday morning vignette so telling. I saw me, and all of us, in Emily's "moment."

Of all our six children, she is the most zealous for the newest worship CDs by worship leaders like Chris Tomlin and Matt Redman. Emily loves attending the *Passion* gatherings. She has helped multiply and mature the worship experiences at her high school. And on Sunday mornings at our church and Sunday evenings at the gatherings of Teen Community Bible Study in our barn, Emily is a hand-raising, soul-engaging worshiper of Jesus.

All these images ran through my heart as I ran to the car, just as the three of them were filling Emily's car with their bodies and less-than-chummy attitudes. "Wait a minute, guys. Before you leave, I need to say something. Emily, *this* morning, this *Monday* morning, you're feeling tired and grumpy. I understand both . . . but everything about your brothers from the way they chew their cereal, to the kind of clothes they are wearing right now seems to be getting under your skin and bugging you. And boys, you haven't exactly endeared yourselves to your sister.

"But *this* moment, this *Monday-morning moment*, is designed for worship just as much as any other moment of the week. I'm not asking you guys to crank up one of your favorite worship CDs right now. And Emily, it *definitely* doesn't mean you're supposed to lift your hands in praise, *off the steering wheel*, as you drive your brothers to school! But we're called to worship Jesus in *everything* we do—including how we love Him on Monday mornings, when we don't get enough sleep, don't get homework finished, don't feel like a group hug, or *whatever*.

"The worship music Jesus longs to hear *this* morning in *this* VW will come from you guys loving and respecting each other. The most important worship any of us *ever* gives Jesus is when we are least aware of it, when we're simply serving Him and one another in the dailiness of life. Now get going, and have a great day. And don't forget, I do love you."

I walked away from that moment thankful for my kids and convicted about the state of worship in my heart and in our generation of contemporary worshipers. In my concerts of recent years, the crowds are more responsive than ever to the portions of the night we set aside for worship singing. It's awesome to see people of all ages and backgrounds so united and engaged when we sing to the Lord. And yet, I'm increasingly concerned about the disparity between lifting our hands in worship and folding our hands when it comes time to serve the Lord when the need for worship servants is most pronounced.

About the time Emily, Caleb, and Will Franklin were pulling up to their school, I had already started writing down these words: *This is a moment made for worshiping, because this is a moment I'm alive. This is a moment I was made to sing, a song of living sacrifice. For every moment that we live and breathe, this is a moment made for worshiping.*

If we're sitting in a classroom or a boardroom, standing in an operating room or on a stage, cooking at the grill, sweeping the floor, changing a diaper . . . wherever we are, *whatever* we're doing, it's to be done as an act of worship. We're to offer up ourselves in that moment as a living sacrifice because of God's great mercy for us in Jesus.

I've never longed so much for the day when we will only, and always, give Jesus the unbroken worship He deserves and delights in. That's why I feel that this chapter, and the next one, may be the most important ones in our book. Please read with care, and join us in reflecting on our most eternal, joyful, and consuming calling—the worship of the living God.

Worship in the Contemporary Church

(Scotty:)

"Tomorrow morning, each of you is to bring me a one-page reflection on the worship service that had the biggest impact on you in the past year. I'll share mine as well. I'm not looking for a technical or theological analysis, but a record of your experience. And you'll get 'busted' if you write more than one double-spaced page. Anybody have any questions? Great, see you all bright and early."

It was the first day of a course I teach during the January term at Covenant Seminary called "Worship in the Contemporary Church." This assignment was a guileless "setup" I put in place to help my eighty-five students take a fresh look at the kind of worship God delights in and desires from us today. Recently, I'd gone through a significant shift in my understanding, and I was eager for this opportunity to process my conclusions with members of the emerging generation. We gathered the next morning at eight o'clock in eight-degree, bone-freezing cold weather.

"Good morning, everyone. Small fires and cuddling will be permitted at your tables until our teeth stop chattering—just kidding. Man, is it cold! OK, how'd you fare in our little exercise? Let's start with hearing about some of your favorite worship service experiences. If you object to having yours read in class, just keep it till the end of the day. Otherwise, please pass them forward. I'll pick a few to share. Here's one from Kevin called, 'Passion 2004.' I'm all for starting our class with a little passion!"

PASSION 2004

" 'This past May, I hooked up with a couple of friends who are seniors at Baylor University. They invited me to attend a worship gathering called *Passion*, which usually draws between ten to twenty thousand college students and young adults. I'd heard about the

Passion events, but figured it'd be a day of "rah-rah" legalistic teaching with a heavy dose of charismatic emotional manipulation. I couldn't have been more wrong.

" 'John Piper preached an incredible sermon, and the music was theologically right on target. Of the eight hours we were together, two or three of them were spent on our faces before the Lord. There was so much singing, and weeping, and repenting . . . and, for the first time in my life, I even danced during worship! I've never experienced anything *remotely* that powerful in my PCA church back in Mississippi. It makes me wonder why we get so hung up on bulletins and formalities.' "

"Thanks Kevin, but did I fail to mention your reports are to be show and tell? I'd welcome a little demonstration of your interpretative dance moves, so if you'd care to step forward, I promise not to report you to Dr. Chapel. Oh well, let's hear another reflection. This one's simply titled, 'Creed,' and is written by Karen."

CREED

" 'My parents divorced just over four years ago, but I'm still new to the holiday visit merry-go-round between families. This year, it worked out best for me to spend Christmas break with my mom and her new husband of six months. They live in Darien, Connecticut, which is a world removed from my Texas heritage.

" 'The main thing I was dreading about Christmas in Connecticut, besides the cold and snow, was being away from my home church, where I've been a part of the praise team since high school. Mom married an Episcopalian believer, though she's deeply rooted in the world of Texas Southern Baptists, but she assured me she felt great about joining my step-dad's church.

" 'I'd never seen the Book of Common Prayer until six weeks ago and, quite honestly, I thought all Episcopalians were theological liberals. But I've just experienced the most incredible Advent season of my life—even my calling it Advent, instead of Christmas, is new for me. I've already been told not all Episcopal churches are like my mom's, but this one is amazing.

" 'What impacted me the most? I loved the interactive rhythms of the liturgy. Hearing the whole congregation engaged in the responsive readings and prayers made it seem like we were all priests worshiping Jesus together. And kneeling several times during worship also touched something deep inside of me. Though I've always been comfortable with people lifting their hands in worship, kneeling is such a powerful physical movement that made the gospel come alive in a fresh and profound way.

" 'Lastly, the Lord's Supper—make that "the Eucharist"—has come alive to me. Back in Texas, we take communion four times a year, and it really isn't that big of a deal. But just *watching* mom's new church family partake of the bread and the wine at the midnight Christmas Eve service with such love, reverence, and joy left me wondering if real Christian worship can even take place *without* the Eucharist. This Baptist girl has come a long way in six weeks.' "

"Whew . . . thank you very much, Karen. I think we've got time for one more. This title alone gets an A—'So Much for Cool'—and is offered by Mark."

So Much for Cool

" 'I'll be graduating this May with an M.Div., and, according to my GPA, with honors. This supposedly indicates that I'm about to be recognized as a "master of divinity," with a capital *M*. The truth is I've never felt *less* like a master of anything, especially divinity.

" 'Last summer, I worked as a pastoral intern at an inner-city church in Chicago. I went there with nine of my best sermons, my PowerBook loaded with film clips and song lyrics, my guitar, and a lot of confidence in my gifts as a worship leader. I *thought* I was going to be working with the college ministry and the church's outreach to the University of Chicago—a "heady" bunch of students who have bought into postmodernity hook, line, and sinker.

" 'But when I got there, the executive pastor told me there'd been a mix-up, and that my internship was designed to provide pastoral care and worship leadership for their summer camp program—a ministry for young adults with the mental and emotional maturity of children between the ages, on the average, of five to eight.

" 'He apologized profusely and offered to cover my expenses and provide some help with my fall tuition. But I stayed . . . and it was the hardest experience in ministry I've ever had, but the most valuable. I learned more about worship from those childlike adults than I ever have anywhere else.

" 'They couldn't understand 5 percent of my sermons—which I quickly put away. They weren't "taken into the third heaven" by my seamless flow of worship songs and the cool DVD clips of nature I programmed and projected onto the screen. In fact, they got bored with that stuff real fast—which irritated me for a while.

" 'But when I *finally* got down on the floor with them, let them hold my hand, acknowledged to the Lord my sense of incompetence and fear of failure, learned *their* simple songs of faith and listened to their life stories, as intently as if great theologians were speaking (which they were) . . . when I got free enough to let them love me, in their own broken ways, I changed as a person.

" 'Right after breakfast on my last day, my new friends gathered around me in a circle and sang to me "Jesus Loves You" . . . and I lost it. I absolutely fell apart. Then they started praying for me, interrupting each other, thanking God for our summer together, and asking protection for my trip home—mixing and matching parts of Bible verses with words of praise choruses. It was the most remarkable worship service I've ever been a part of. *They* are the masters of divinity.' "

"Mark, I'm supposed to 'bust' you for going over our one-page limit, but I'd really want to hug you. Thanks for being so vulnerable with us." A number of damp eyes in the class gave visible affirmation of this same sentiment.

"I wish we could spend the rest of the morning just reading all your reflection papers, but we've got so little time and so much syllabus to cover, so if you'd turn . . ."

"Mr. Smith, excuse the interruption . . ."

Yes! I said to myself. *Somebody's taking the bait!* One of my students in the far left corner (not a political statement) was waving his hand, trying his best to get my attention. I was hoping for this moment, so I could sneak in through the back door with a challenge to our conventional way of thinking about worship.

"You said you'd share your favorite worship service of the past year with us too. Were you planning to do that now or later?"

"Fair enough. We've got a lot of material to cover, but now's as good a time as any for me to share my story."

A Grain Offering

"My story took place last February during my first visit to Ethiopia. Seven of us from Christ Community flew into Addis Ababa from Cape Town, South Africa, before driving several hours south on the next day to a missionary compound, operated by SIM, formerly the Sudan Interior Mission. This place gave new meaning to the phrase, 'in the middle of nowhere.' We enjoyed a much-needed Saturday evening of good food and rest, after the grueling travel schedule of the previous twenty-four hours.

"The next day, we divided into four different groups and spent the morning leading services of worship in several small churches under the oversight of SIM—an experience I will *never* forget. I was asked to accompany a SIM missionary couple and preach in a village church that would 'require a little walking,' as they told/warned me.

"After traveling thirty minutes in a four-wheel-drive Land Rover, *as far as it could safely navigate*, we began our walk—which turned out to be more like a Boy Scout initiation hike. Forty minutes later, and about a thousand feet higher above sea level, we came to a village that connected me with the *National Geographic* magazines of my youth . . . and to Genesis 2:25, which speaks of the day when Adam and Ever were clothe-less and shameless, if you get the picture.

"The presiding elder warmly welcomed us at the outskirts of the village, and then hurried us along to a thatched hut—I'd say, of

146

about twenty feet square. Once inside, we were greeted by nineteen sets of the most beautiful eyes you have ever seen—that's counting two infants and a couple of very friendly dogs.

"The service of worship began with an older gentleman offering prayer—and he did so with such humility and joy that I was blessed, even though I could not understand a word he said. After the 'Amen!', another brother started singing a beautiful, simple melody, but halfway into the first verse, it was as though a small vocal orchestra suddenly materialized and turned that dirt-floor hut into a majestic cathedral.

"Living in Nashville, I hear a ton of great worship music—covering the full gamut of artistic style. But nothing like this! I wish you could have heard God being praised through the intricate harmonies and complex rhythms of this unlikely ensemble of toothless men, nursing mothers, and half-naked children. I was awestruck.

"It was *easy* to preach after that 'warm-up.' I told my interpreter to translate, 'trash,' or transform my message any way he wanted: to most effectively communicate the matchless love of Jesus to this little band of the beloved. What a testimony to the power of the gospel that service of worship was! "But that's just the introduction. *Now* I can tell you about the most meaningful worship service I've experienced in the past year. It happened the next day.

"We loaded into our vehicles early the next morning and headed toward the community of Tufa, which we affectionately renamed 'too far,' as in, 'This place is "too far" from *everything*.' Riding shotgun in the lead car, I got the first glimpse of our destination. Two things came into view as we approached: a huge pile of white grain bags, with dozens of burros grazing close by; and then, on a small rise behind them—looking like a snapshot from the New Testament—there were three or four hundred Ethiopian villagers sitting down in orderly fashion, obviously anticipating our arrival with great joy.

"For the next seven or eight hours, we distributed several tons of seventy-five-pound bags of wheat to the families of Tufa, a Muslim community of about 3,000 members that was devastated by the famines that have led to the deaths of thousands of Ethiopians. Our church family had recently taken a love offering during a service of worship, in response to an earnest appeal from one of our members. That one gift of 40,000 was enough to feed the whole community of Tufa for *half a year*.

"I'd never *really* experienced the cruel reality of starvation and malnutrition until that day. Nor had I understood the grave significance of the petition in the Lord's Prayer for 'daily bread.' I wish you could have seen the expressions on the faces of mothers as we hoisted bags of grain onto the backs of their gentle burros. Grateful tears flowed freely, generated by the relief of not having to put their children to bed crying with hunger for the next six months.

"Dusk approached, and we were exhausted and exhilarated at the same time. The exhaustion came from the sheer physical labor, and the exhilaration came from the worship service of the day. *Never* have I experienced worship service more profound, engaging, and gospel-driven—not just in the past year, but *ever*.

"As we loaded into our vehicles and began to drive away, a young woman with a baby 'papoosed' against her chest started waving both of her arms to get us to stop. She came up to the driver's side of our car and spoke a few words to Nicodemus, a SIM missionary. He turned to us and said, 'She asked me to tell you, "thank you" . . . for saving her life.' Stunned, we offered a polite, 'You're so very welcome.' But for the next several minutes of our ride home, we said nothing to one another—each of us staring out his window, silenced by the profound implications of the benediction just spoken over us."

SERVICE OF WORSHIP OR WORSHIP SERVICE?

A couple of hands went up in the classroom. "Yes, Sally," I answered.

"I don't mean to be rude, but didn't you leave something out? Maybe I missed it, but I don't remember you telling us about the actual worship service at the food distribution site. It must have been awesome. How'd you pull it off? You mentioned it was a Muslim community . . . I'm guessing you, or somebody else, preached the gospel. So, who led the worship? And did anybody come to Christ?"

"Thank you, thank you, thank you, Sally! I was counting on *somebody* in class coming through for me, and Sally, it's you! This is the fourth time I've taught this course at Covenant, and I've deliberately designed it to be a forum that welcomes dialog, new ideas about worship, and an openness to change. But, I join you this year as the one who's gone through a significant change of my own. Hopefully, it reflects a greater sensitivity to God's design and delights in worship.

"The reflection paper I asked you to write was designed for this very moment. As I shared my 'reflection,' did any of you notice I used two different phrases while telling my story? When describing the gathering in the village hut—or mud-and-straw cathedral!—I spoke of the *service of worship* we enjoyed together, referring to the hour and a half we spent in corporate adoration of God through music, the Scriptures, and prayer. But when recounting the food distribution in Tufa, I used the phrase *worship service* to describe what took place.

"I'm compelled by the Scriptures to make this, what I believe to be, a most critical and important distinction between these two phrases. For me, the phrase *worship service* is now synonymous with a more familiar phrase, *The Christian life*. What is the Christian life? It's *worship service*—a commitment to declare God's glory and worth in *everything* we say, think, and do—in every sphere of life, including in our *services of worship*! *Worship service* is doxological discipleship; it's living in God's Story for God's glory with God's joy!

"Is this a mere quibbling over words, the musings of a pastor with far too much discretionary time on his hands? Absolutely not! I believe we've misunderstood the 'call to worship' *big time*. We've relegated worship to one area of our lives, but God designed worship to regulate *all* areas of our lives. Our understanding of worship is broken, our worship *itself* is broken, and *we* are broken worshipers. But Jesus has come to restore all things, including the worship of God.

"From the beginning, in Creation, God created His world and His people for the declaring of His worth. The English word *worship* means exactly that, "to declare worth." Think for a moment: where were Adam and Eve supposed to go in the Garden of Eden to declare God's worth, to worship Him? Where was the chapel, temple, sanctuary, or worship center located? What sacred space was set apart for them to engage in services of worship?

"There wasn't any! Why? Because *everything* Adam and Eve did was meant to be music in God's ears—joyful expressions of His glory and goodness. Whether they were tending the Garden, playing with the animals, making love as husband and wife, walking with and communing with God in the 'cool of the day,' creating culture from the raw materials of creation, eating, drinking, studying the beauty of a single flower, executing dominion over God's creation . . . *everything* God designed for Adam and Eve was meant to be celebrated as an act of worship! Nothing was designated as being a non-worship act.

"Now fast-forward to the *last* picture of worship we are given in the Scriptures, which is the first glimpse we have of the eternal future of worship. In Revelation 21:22–23, we read, 'And I saw no temple in the city, for its temple is the Lord God the Almighty and the Lamb. And the city has no need of sun or moon to shine on it, for the glory of God gives it light, and its lamp is the Lamb.'

"Why do you suppose John *looked* for a temple in the new heaven and new earth? No doubt, to draw dramatic attention to the complete absence of the temple in the new heaven and new earth. John wasn't really expecting to *find* the temple. Rather, he wants us to ponder the profound implications of the temple-less worship of eternity! John envisioned the day when God's worship will once again be the comprehensive celebration in all of life and no longer an important component of our broken lives. This is the end of the important part of God's Story, which tells the story of temple worship.

"The place of the temple worship in God's Story points toward the day when God and the Lamb, themselves, will be the everlasting 'house of worship' . . . the sphere in which all glory, praise, and honor will be given. Ever since the Exodus, the temple represented God's gracious commitment to restore His *broken people*, His *broken worship*, and His *broken creation*. Particular *services of worship* were decreed by God in response to the effects of the Fall. When the *worship service* of Creation was corrupted and broken, *services of worship* became the promise and provision of the restoration of true worship one day in the New Creation.

"The people of God gathered in the temple for the appointed *services of worship*—times of confession, prayer, sacrifice, and priestly ministrations. Israel's temple was a proclamation of the gospel—by substitutionary death, the sins of God's people could be covered and relationship with Him renewed. But the blood of animals offered by sacrifice in the temple all pointed to the day when Jesus, the Lamb of God, came and shed His blood upon the Cross, as the perfect sacrifice of atonement—the fulfillment of all Old Testament bloody sacrifices—*the ultimate service of worship* and *worship service*.

"With Jesus' resurrection and the outpouring of the Holy Spirit on the day of Pentecost, *services of worship* were transformed. The temple in Jerusalem, and Jerusalem itself, ceased to be a point of focus for God's worship. Followers of Jesus were instructed that God is seeking true worshipers, not great worship. He is seeking a particular people, not a particular liturgy—a people who will worship Him in truth and spirit, wherever they are.

"*Services of worship* must now demonstrate a radical break with dependence upon the priesthood of Israel's temple. For, in Christ, every follower of Jesus has become a living stone of a new *living* temple, not tied to physical location. And the entire body of Christ has been made a priesthood of believers—each of us having the privilege of access into the Holy of Holies and confidence to come boldly to a throne of grace.

"As a kingdom of priests, we are expected to mature as God's worshipers in our *services of worship*, while celebrating the Lord Jesus' person and work through the ministry of the Word, the sacraments, prayer, praise, and fellowship. But we are also charged to incrementally restore God's broken worship by offering ourselves to God as 'living sacrifices,' as a people who accept the calling to the lifestyle of *worship service*, wherever God has placed us or will send us.

"We're to make music pleasing to God's ears and heart in *everything* we think, say, and do, remembering the Garden of Eden and anticipating our life in the new heaven and new earth. For in John's vision of future worship, God Himself will have become the temple—all shadows and symbols will give way to their fulfillment. Once again and forever, *all* of life will be lived as *worship service*—no one act, action, or attitude will be more holy, sacred, or worshipful than another!

"Now here's my question: since this is how God first designed us to worship Him in the Garden of Eden, and since this is how we will worship Him when sin is completely eradicated, what are the implications for how we are to worship God *today*?

"I'm now convinced that we've placed an inordinate and unbiblical emphasis on our *services of worship*, largely to the exception of *worship service*. And it makes the ongoing '*worship wars*' over musical styles and liturgical elements seem pretty silly and petty to me.

"As a pastor who has had the enviable joy of having unlimited musical resources and creative personnel to create 'great worship,' trust me that building emotionally moving services of worship is a *snap* compared to the work and cost of cultivating *worship service* and worship servants. This was underscored recently when I attended concerts by Bruce Springsteen and James Taylor. Though I thoroughly enjoyed both of these artists, it felt kind of eerie to notice the similarities between these concerts and many worship events I've experienced recently.

"At both of these concerts, there was humble, 'charismatic,' upfront leadership, amazing musicianship, a heightened whole-audience response when favorite songs were played, physical movement of congregants (I mean concert-goers), a sense of connecting and community, moments of climax and resolve. And, at the end, everyone left with a sense of having been thoroughly engaged and satisfied. It felt, well, like many contemporary worship gatherings—a group of satisfied consumers going home. "But if what we call 'worship,' in our churches, can be duplicated by secular entertainment without any reliance on the Holy Spirit or reference to Jesus, then we must grieve and repent. Wouldn't you agree?

"This week, I want you to think with me, pray with me, and debate with me concerning the implications of all of this. If my understanding is correct, then I should return your reflection papers and make you start all over again . . . because you misunderstood the assignment. I asked for a paper on *worship service*, not your favorite *service of worship*. Not to worry, I'm not going to do that!

"In what sense, then, was my time at the food distribution site *worship service*? If worship is anything, it is giving to Jesus that which He desires and deserves. So what 'sacrifice of praise' does Jesus desire? What is 'music' to Jesus' ears? Let me read some familiar words with you, and I challenge you to hear them in a new way—as a liturgy for *worship service*.

"Come, you who are blessed by my Father, inherit the kingdom prepared for you from the foundation of the world. For I was hungry and you gave me food, I was thirsty and you gave me drink, I was a stranger and you welcomed me, I was naked and you clothed me, I was sick and you visited me, I was in prison and you came to me." Then the righteous will answer him, saying, "Lord, when did we see you hungry and feed you, or thirsty and give you drink? And when did we see you a stranger and welcome you, or naked and clothe you? And when did we see you sick or in prison and visit you?" And the King will answer them, "Truly, I say to you, as you did it to one of the least of these my brothers, you did it to me" (Matthew 25:34–40).

"Based on this scripture, here's a suggested 'set list' of praise music Jesus has established for all time. Let's get the praise team and the choir working hard on these worship songs:

- Feed the hungry.
- Quench the thirsty.
- Welcome strangers.
- Clothe the naked.
- Care for the sick.
- Minister to prisoners.

"Think about these images, and we'll pick up at this point after our lunch break. Stay warm, and please get back to class on time!
"By the way, I'll be more than glad to answer any questions this

155

morning session has generated, but I'd very much appreciate your writing them out for me. I'll stay around a few minutes, if you want to take a minute and write something out, or just hand them to me a few minutes before we resume at one o'clock. Thanks."

9 RESTORING BROKEN WORSHIPERS

"Please, please, please only You, only You
Please, please, please take my heart and make it true
Let everything I say and everything I do
Please, please only You
This is what it means to be
The reason why I live and breathe
To know that I am totally existing for Your pleasure"
— SCC "Please Only You"

(SCOTTY):

Welcome back, everybody. Grab a cup of coffee, if you need it. I don't want to be interrupting any afternoon naps! Let's pick up where we left off. The distinction I'm making between *services of worship* and *worship service* seems to be pushing some buttons, as evidenced by some of the spirited questions turned in. Here's a good example: 'Would you please provide more background to your *worship service / services of worship* continuum? I'm not sure I get it, or agree with it, but can you help me understand a little better how you got there? What are the implications for the contemporary church, and how is this paradigm doable?'

"Basically, I 'got there' with two important influences. First of all, I began studying the Bible less as an encyclopedia of specific doctrines, and more as the unfolding of one great Story—God's commitment to redeem a people and His creation through His Son, Jesus. This led me to take a close look at how different themes are revealed and developed *historically* and *progressively* through God's story of redemption . . . beginning with the day Jesus created the first heaven and first earth, until the day He will return to create the *new* heaven and *new* earth.

"With respect to the worship, I began studying the past, present, and future of worship from *God's* perspective, which led me to wrestle questions such as: what was God's original design for His worship? What has happened to his worship as a result of the intrusion of sin and death? How is God's worship being progressively redeemed through the work of Jesus? And how will we worship God perfectly and eternally after the second coming of Jesus?

"Pondering these questions pushed me toward the second major influence God used to reshape my understanding of worship: the Book of Revelation. I've carried on a long-standing wrestling match with Revelation since I became a Christian in the late '60s. Though it confused and even frightened me as a young believer, three and a half decades later, Revelation has become one of my three favorite books in the Bible—probably because of its story structure, and the visual and auditory imagery the apostle John used in writing His masterpiece; but, most *definitely*, because of its emphasis on worship and the centrality of the work of Jesus.

"Today, I think of Revelation as 'The Chronicles of Jesus and His Victory in the Real Worship War.' Because the *main* story that John is telling is the story of God's worship—the past, present, and future of the most defining and contested category in *all* of life, and Jesus' central role in this story.

"In particular, God has used the last two chapters of Revelation to radically reorient my understanding of worship and everything else. Since God has been pleased to give us a glorious glimpse, however partial, of the fully restored world of the new heaven and new earth, doesn't it stand to reason that He intends for us to become as familiar as possible with our destiny? The more we fill our hearts with a vision of the perfect world of *tomorrow*, the better equipped we will be for living as agents of hope and restoration in the broken world of *today*! And the better acquainted we are with God's perfected worship, the more faithfully we will worship Him, and help others worship Him today.

"For example, I was far better equipped to converse about Switzerland and introduce friends to my favorite country in the world after I had actually *been* there a few times for myself. Two viewings of the movie *Heidi*, a few yodeling lessons, a pair of lederhosen, and a love for Swiss chocolate don't make you a Swiss tour guide; any more than knowing a few Chris Tomlin worship songs, mastering four or five guitar chords, loving Jesus, and having an audience make you a worship leader. We've got to *be* worshipers before we can *lead* worship. And this involves becoming far more familiar and engaged with God *Himself* and with *His* design and delights in worship.

"Thus, when I started spending time immersing myself in John's vision of the present worship in heaven and the perfected worship of eternity, all kinds of alarms, whistles, and lights started going off. I stopped trying to fit bits of Revelation into *my* worship experience, and began to enter more fully into God's Story, and into *His* experience of worship. I'm convinced that the final book of the Bible concerns itself chiefly with God's worship, as it was *meant to be* and as it *will be* one day, so that we will worship Him more faithfully in *this* day—*our* day.

"When John wrote about worship in Revelation, he wasn't engaging in debates, nor was he even thinking about questions of art, style, liturgy, or musical preferences in the *services of worship*. Rather, John was concerned with the real meaning of worship—with *worship service* . . . that is, with helping the young church in Asia Minor know how to live faithfully as the betrothed Bride of Jesus on a day-in-and-day-out basis in *this* world, while longing for the wedding day in the new heaven and new earth.

"*These* are to be the main concerns of followers of Jesus: How do we adore and serve the One who has lived and died to make us His Bride? How can we possibly offer an adequate response to Jesus for the grace and love He has lavished upon us? What expressions of love and faithfulness does He desire from us? How do we worship Him well?

"Indeed, Revelation doesn't present worship as a component, even the most important component of the Christian life. For the original recipients of the letter, worship is assumed to be the one category carrying implications for *every* aspect of their lives—politically, economically, culturally, and physically. Worship was an issue forced upon them, not merely by their cultural heritage or religious preferences, but by the dark powers of the Roman world.

"Michael Wilcock put it like this: 'The Roman Empire, powerful in many senses, exercised one particular power which became a cause of great trials to the early Christians. The growing practice of *emperor worship* meant that an increasing number of believers were required publicly to make the fateful choice between Caesar and Christ. Every age has its equivalent of a Christian's true allegiance; for them, it meant actual persecution and the threat of martyrdom.'[1]

"Emperor worship, in *any* form, collided with the central confession and defining story line of the church: 'Jesus is LORD!' We belong to our beloved Bridegroom. His banner over us is love. Though we are called to live as good citizens and to become the best neighbors possible—participating in *every* aspect of life in the community and culture—Christians are, *above all else*, the Bride of Jesus.

"Our hearts, along with everything else, have already been fully spoken for. Revelation doesn't present worship as something we do to grow spiritually. Rather, it's the consuming whole-life response of the ill-deserving prostitute who has become the wife and queen of the King of kings—Jesus Christ!

"Through believing the gospel, we are already legally married to Jesus, though we await our wedding day. As His loving Bride, we should be passionate about Jesus' passions and involved in His interests. And since our Bridegroom has committed Himself to ridding the world of every semblance and effect of sin and death, and to the making of all *things* new . . . well, you get the picture, don't you? Where Jesus is, *we* are to be. What Jesus is doing, *we* are to be doing. *This* is the real *worship war*—demonstrating our love and adoration for Jesus *all the time* and in *every* sphere of life. Not just in our *services of worship*, but by our *worship service*. We're on a world-transforming mission with Jesus, not on a Saturday night date!

"Think about it. How would you like it if all your fiancée wanted to do was to cuddle and kiss, without demonstrating a commitment or desire to be involved with you in any *other* aspect of your life. How do you suppose you'd feel? On second thought, that's the wrong question to ask the unmarried men in the class! Forget the period of engagement; let's talk about marriage itself, after the honeymoon.

"SEX AND WORSHIP!" I saw a few nodding heads. "That ought to wake you up! What do sex and worship have in common? Sexual intimacy was designed by God to be a passionate celebration of the commitment and companionship shared between a husband and wife. Sex was *never* meant to be a *substitute* for these relational riches, and God never intended sex to be used to mend a relationship, as in 'make-up sex.' It's just as unhealthy and destructive to misuse the gift of sexual intimacy within marriage as outside of this covenant relationship.

"There are strong parallels between worship life and married life. In the most holy and joyful sense, *individual acts* and *corporate services of worship* are to *worship service* what sexual intimacy is to a healthy marriage—a passionate celebration of a whole-life commitment and other-centered love. It's just as easy to misuse worship in our relationship with Jesus as it is for spouses to misuse sex in marriage. And the results are just as unhealthy, and, at times, just as destructive.

"Are there any questions? I hope I haven't offended any of you. Whew, it suddenly got pretty hot in here. Let's take a ten-minute stretch break, and then we'll segue into our next worship continuum, which I think will clarify many of the issues still very much on the table."

THE KIND OF WORSHIPERS THE FATHER SEEKS

"Before the break, I mentioned we still had some things on the table . . . literally, we've got a ton of goodies on the table just to my right. Please help yourselves, and then turn in your Bibles to John 4, which is the chapter I believe to be the most pivotal statement on worship given to us in the New Testament. Think about this phrase while you're settling in: 'seeker-sensitive worship.' That ought to get a rise out of you guys.

"The author of the fourth gospel is the same John who gave us the Book of Revelation. Both volumes reveal Jesus' passion for restoring God's broken worship and His broken worshipers. It's worth noting that Jesus delivered His most detailed and complete teaching on worship to a most unlikely candidate—a very broken Samaritan woman.

"As the story begins in John 4:1, we are told that Jesus and His disciples were heading back to Galilee from Judea, and that they 'had' to pass through Samaria. But it was providence, not expedience that compelled Jesus to route His men through Samaria to the small town of Sychar. Typically, Jews would avoid *any* encounter with the people of Samaria. Arriving around noon, and weary from their travels, the disciples went into the plaza to buy some food while Jesus sat down to relax beside a public well.

"Against custom and convention, a Samaritan woman came by herself to draw water in the middle of the day. This was usually a chore accomplished early in the morning, before the scorching heat of the sun intensified the effort required for this daily necessity. Her timing indicates there were reasons she preferred to avoid the usual early morning crowd.

"Jesus also showed His disregard for conventionality by cordially asking the startled woman for a drink of water. She was shocked because Jesus was crossing assumed national and religious boundaries. Jews typically despised the Samaritans. They considered them *half-breeds*—an 'impure' and 'unclean' people group formed when the ten northern tribes of Israel were taken into captivity by the Assyrians and forced to intermarry with pagan Gentiles.

"But Jesus was also violating the prevailing attitude and social mores toward women. A Jewish rabbi would not consider speaking to a woman the way Jesus did, with such familiarity and respect at a public gathering place. Understandably, she responded with a hint of sarcasm and disbelief: 'How can *you* ask *me* for a drink?' At that moment, the gates of grace flew open, and Jesus loved this throwaway-woman as no one ever had."

Jesus answered her, "If you knew the gift of God, and who it is that is saying to you, 'Give me a drink,' you would have asked him, and he would have given you living water." The woman said to him, "Sir, you have nothing to draw water with, and the well is deep. Where do you get that living water? Are you greater than our father Jacob? He gave us the well and drank from it himself, as did his sons and his livestock." Jesus said to her, "Everyone who drinks of this water will be thirsty again, but whoever drinks of the water that I will give him will never be thirsty forever. The water that I will give him will become in him a spring of water welling up to eternal life." The woman said to him, "Sir, give me this water, so that I will not be thirsty or have to come here to draw water." Jesus said to her, "Go, call your husband, and come here." The woman answered him, "I have no husband." Jesus said to her, "You are right in saying, 'I have no husband'; for you have had five husbands, and the one you now have is not your husband. What you have said is true." The woman said to him, "Sir, I perceive that you are a prophet. Our fathers worshiped on this mountain, but you say that in Jerusalem is the place where people ought to worship." Jesus said to her, "Woman, believe me, the hour is coming when neither on this mountain nor in Jerusalem will you worship the Father. You worship what you do not know; we worship what we know, for salvation is from the Jews. But the hour is coming, and is now here, when the true worshipers will worship the Father in spirit and truth, for the Father is seeking such people to worship him. God is spirit, and those who worship him must worship in spirit and truth." The woman said to him, "I know that Messiah is coming (he who is called Christ). When he comes, he will tell us all things." Jesus said to her, "I who speak to you am he" (John 4:10–26).

"It's hard for us to appreciate the glory and grace revealed in this story. For Jesus to give this particular broken woman such unparalleled insight into history and biblical theology of worship is comparable to Michelangelo giving painting lessons to a homeless thief; or William Shakespeare sharing the history and skills of sonnet writing with a home-wrecking alcoholic; or Tiger Woods helping a young streetwalking prostitute develop the mechanics of a flawless and effortless golf swing. This is a story of the *heart* of worship, before it is a revelation of the *art* of worship. Let's start by identifying some of the more important themes in the passage. This material is not in your syllabus, so you may want to take notes."

God the Father Is Into Seeker-Sensitive Worship

"A few moments ago, I threw out the phrase 'seeker-sensitive worship.' What do you think about that? Does the Bible encourage *seeker-sensitive* worship? Absolutely! But not the kind we generally think about. Take a close look at this passage. The main seeker identified in the story is God Himself, and our calling is to gladly give Him *anything* He desires from us.

"Think about it. Don't you find it remarkable that God is 'seeking' *anything*—the One who has *everything* and needs *nothing* is revealed as a *seeker*. And John tells us, in verse 23, that He is seeking with a definite worship agenda in mind."

God the Father Is Seeking True Worshipers, Not Great Worship

"Though it has become an accepted part of our contemporary worship-speak, only God has the right to say, 'Awesome worship!' or, 'I didn't really get anything out of the worship today.' After all, it's *His* worship, not ours. That we experience joy and pleasure in the worship of God is appropriate and a profound privilege; but it is *God's* pleasure that we are to be most concerned about.

"The more I study the unfolding history of worship in the Bible, the more I'm forced to conclude that many times when we're *enjoying* worship, God is barely *enduring* it. The prophet Amos illustrates this truth powerfully and painfully."

I hate, I despise your feasts, and I take no delight in your solemn assemblies. *Even though you offer me your burnt offerings and grain offerings, I will not accept them; and the peace offerings of your fattened animals, I will not look upon them.* Take away from me the noise of your songs; to the melody of your harps I will not listen. *But let justice roll down like waters, and righteousness like an ever-flowing stream* (Amos 5:21–24; emphasis mine).

"Eugene Peterson's paraphrase of the same passage, in *The Message*, connects God's rebuke to our contemporary worship culture."

I can't stand your religious meetings. *I'm fed up with your conferences and conventions. I want nothing to do with your religious projects, your pretentious slogans and goals. I'm sick of your fund-raising schemes, your public relations and image making.* I've had all I can take of your noisy ego-music. *When was the last time you sang to me? Do you know what I want? I want justice—oceans of it. I want fairness—rivers of it. That's what I want. That's all I want* (emphasis added).

"Amos confirms that God *does* have an opinion about our worship music, and he also confirms that God prefers the worship of social justice to the worship of 'noisy ego-music.'

"In His conversation with the Samaritan woman, Jesus doesn't say God is seeking great worship; rather, the Father is seeking *true worshipers*. In fact, there isn't a single verse in the Bible that says God is looking for, or desiring, great *services of worship*. But there are *plenty* of scriptures declaring His intent to have *faithful worshipers—worship servants*. God is not primarily seeking a particular liturgy, but a peculiar people—a people who will worship Him *in spirit and in truth*.

"Pause and think with me for a moment: can you see in this text how Jesus has declared war on most of *our* worship wars? Jesus is telling us that worship is not something we merely *do* as Christians, it is who we are to *become* through the gospel! God addresses the issue of broken worship by coming after broken worshipers, like this Samaritan woman, and the rag-tag gang of disciples with whom Jesus surrounded Himself . . . and you and me.

"This encounter with the Samaritan woman reminds us that the history of worship is God creating a family to know, love, and serve Him as a merciful Father. But what, then, does it mean to worship Him 'in spirit and truth' [vv. 23–24]. What did Jesus mean by these theologically loaded words, and what was their significance for the Samaritan woman?"

The Father Is Seeking Spirit-Filled Worshipers, Not Spirit-Filled Worship

"When Jesus offered this broken woman 'living water,' He wasn't just speaking metaphorically. This whole story is built around the theme of *things essential for life*. The disciples went into town for bread, and the Samaritan woman came to a well for water. We must have both of these for life to be sustained.

"But when Jesus offered living water to the Samaritan woman, He was offering her *eternal* life—which can only be created and sustained by the Holy Spirit. Physical life cannot be *sustained* without H_2O, and *eternal* life cannot be *attained* apart from the gift of the Holy Spirit. By the power of the Holy Spirit, God enables us to respond to Jesus' offer of living water—the only water that can quench the deepest thirst of our hearts. To worship God 'in spirit,' therefore, is to be made spiritually alive by Jesus and to receive the free gift of eternal life.

"But what exactly did Jesus mean by 'eternal life'? In the unfolding drama of God's Story, eternal life is revealed not primarily as a *quantity* of life—that is, the everlasting blessings of heaven—but rather, it's a *quality* of life. *Eternal life* describes the age of cosmic renewal that the promised Messiah was to inaugurate when He arrived—the 'Messianic age of restoration,' the transforming dominion of the true King: Jesus.

"Therefore, to receive the Spirit is to become a participant in the 'powers of the age to come' (Hebrews 6:5) and the 'firstfruits' of the new-creation world (Romans 8:18-25). The Holy Spirit doesn't just make our *services of worship* lively and powerful. He primarily brings us into a whole new realm and a way of life called *eternal* life, which is a life of *worship service*."

The Father Is Seeking True Worshipers, Not Just True Worship
"What then, does it mean to worship 'in truth'? Jesus provides the life-giving Spirit, and He also brings us the ultimate revelation about *all* things. He speaks God's truth because He *is* the Truth. Both are essential to our becoming true worshipers—*worship servants*."

A True Worshiper Is Someone Who Accepts the Truth About Jesus
"Look closely at Jesus' response to the Samaritan woman. What a revelation of grace! 'If you knew the gift of God, and who it is that

is saying to you, "Give me a drink," you would have asked him, and he would have given you living water' (v. 10). Jesus makes it clear that it is *impossible* to be a true worshiper and have a false or untrue assessment of Jesus. We only become true worshipers by receiving what Jesus alone can give: eternal life. And what right does Jesus have to offer eternal life and speak God's truth? As this story unfolds, Jesus reveals the basis of his authority.

"Later in the conversation, the Samaritan woman expressed the hope that one day the Messiah would arrive and *explain everything*—to which Jesus responded, 'I who speak to you am he' (v. 25). Jesus is the promised Messiah, the true King, and the Savior of the world! To worship God 'in truth' will *always* require that we look to Jesus as the final Word about worship—and everything else. As Messiah, Jesus is the substance who fulfills all 'shadow[s] of good things to come' (Hebrews 10:1), including all the elements of Old Testament worship."

A True Worshiper Learns to Distinguish Between the Word of the Father and the Traditions of "the Fathers"

"In our class of eighty-five students this week, we have ten different denominations represented. And from the one-page assignment I had you write, we have at least four times that many opinions about 'great worship.' Jesus' conversation with the Samaritan woman is so important for that very reason. How are we to discern the difference between essential and nonessential when it comes to the worship of God?

"When the Samaritan woman said, 'Our fathers worshiped on this mountain,' she was speaking for every one of us who comes from a particular worship tradition. Each of us tends to appeal to 'our fathers'—our favorite teachers and the fathers of our worship traditions. But only Jesus can tell us which worship mountains are worth fighting for, and which ones are mere mole hills and nothing more than personal traditions of the fathers of ancient, prevailing, and popular cultures. Both the Samaritan fathers and the Jewish fathers were in need of fresh revelation from their heavenly Father, and it was given through Jesus."

A True Worshiper Is Someone Who Accepts the Truth About Himself
"A true worshiper—the kind the Father is seeking—acknowledges his sin and brokenness. When Jesus told the Samaritan woman to 'go, call your husband, and come here' (v.16), he was exposing the insatiable thirst of her heart and the wrong ways she had been trying to quench this thirst—with the 'broken cistern' of human relationships.

"According to Jesus, she was currently in either a promiscuous or adulterous relationship—after already having five husbands! Whether those were actual marriages or not we don't know, but we *do* know this woman tried her best to slake her thirst through intimate relationships with men. Jesus wasn't seeking to condemn her, but to save her and to quench this woman's thirst forever.

IF YOU WANT TO LEAD . . .

"Now . . . *finally!* The second major worship continuum I promised you: a true worshiper is a *lead worshiper* and not merely a *worship leader.* "The disciples returned from their bread hunt just after Jesus declared Himself to be the Messiah to the Samaritan woman, and probably right after she received eternal life from Him. Let's put her story into perspective. She was labeled a half-breed by the nation of Israel, broken by a lifestyle of sequential affairs with men, and shamed to the point of coming alone in the midday sun to draw water by which to survive. But then she met Jesus, and the impact was immediate and liberating!

"She left her water jug at the well and hurried off to town, humbly and joyfully proclaiming to her people, 'Come, see a man who told me all that I ever did. Can this be the Christ?' (v. 29). Her question wasn't intended to express doubt—just the opposite. She, who shamefully crept to Jacob's well alone, was now extending a loud public invitation to the people of the town—friends and strangers alike—to come and discover Jesus for themselves. Jesus is God's Messiah, the promised Savior who welcomes, receives, and forgives adulteresses and broken worshipers just like her . . . just like us.

"In this amazing story, we are given a picture of the kind of worshipers the Father is seeking. The Samaritan woman is Exhibit A. Notice that we don't find her closing her eyes in adoration, lifting her hands in praise, dancing before the Lord, or even laying prostrate before Him. We aren't given even a tiny glimpse of this woman in a *service of worship*, even though she later would have obediently and gladly engaged in such.

"But what we are given is of far greater value. This woman may have never become a worship leader in her church, but she did become what Jesus desires to make of *all of us*—she became a *lead worshiper* in her community! In the streets, at the market, in her neighborhood . . . maybe even with her friends at the local brothel, where her brokenness was *most* manifest. This precious woman could now cry with bold humility and kingdom joy, 'Come, see a man who told me *everything* I ever did. And He loves and has forgiven me . . . and He will do the same for you!'

"Oh, the power and freedom of the gospel that enables us to draw attention away from ourselves unto Jesus. Can't you just hear her saying, 'All the dark, foolish, cruel, and selfish things I ever did, *this* man knows about and yet loves me. You've got to meet Him'? I can feel the refreshing splash of living water as her words land on my heart.

"And meet Him, the townspeople did. 'Many Samaritans from that town believed in Him because of the woman's testimony' (v. 39). Her impact as a *lead worshiper* was profound. 'It is no longer because of what you said that we believe, for we have heard for ourselves, and we know that this is indeed the Savior of the world' (v. 42).

"What is a *lead worshiper*? Someone who makes much of Jesus *wherever* they are, and with whatever they have: in their hearts and with their hands. In their vocation and on their vacations. When tuning a guitar or cleaning a tuna. By caring for an invalid or when validating a parking ticket. By adopting an orphan or enjoying a sunset. As a professional worship leader or as a tone-deaf investment planner. When visiting a prisoner or polishing an antique.

"The highest worship we can offer God in this life is to live, love, sing, pray, study, spend, invest, and sacrifice in ways that will call as much attention as possible to the glory and grace of Jesus Christ. Make much of Jesus . . . make much of Jesus as lead worshipers and as worship leaders. Make much of Jesus in *services of worship* and by *worship service*. If God has gifted, called, and anointed you to be a *worship leader*, then, first and foremost, be a *lead worshiper* by making much of Jesus in all things."

LEAD WORSHIPERS IN EVERY AREA OF LIFE

"In view of the perfected worship of the new heaven and new earth, let's pray for a generation of *lead worshipers* to emerge, not just to honor the Lord in our *services of worship*, but for *worship service* in every sphere of life, culture, and community. We need lead worshipers in social justice, in education, in pastoring and church vocations, in business and economics, in the arts, in environmental studies, in science and technology, in cross-cultural evangelism and missions, in urban development, in politics and law, in medicine, in international relations, in publishing and communication, in farming and nutrition, in counseling and caregiving . . . in all things. As Abraham Kuyper, former prime minister of the Netherlands, said, 'There is not one square inch of the universe about which Jesus Christ does not say, "Mine!" ' "

FOR FURTHER REFLECTION

As you digest what may be a paradigm shift in your understanding of worship, consider its ongoing history, as seen in the past, present, and future.

1. Remember the Original Design of Worship

Everything in creation perfectly reflected God's glory and declared His immeasurable worth. Adam and Eve lived all of life to the glory of God and for the pleasure of God. They offered the ceaseless praise of worship service in their work, play, relationship, and direct communion with God.

2. Ponder the Present Purpose of Worship

Because of the intrusion of sin and death into creation, everything is broken, including worship service. In His generosity, God designed and provided services of worship that show, tell, and celebrate His Story of cosmic restoration through Jesus. These services of worship initially were centered in the tabernacle and then the temple of Jerusalem.

Temple worship was fulfilled by the life, death, and resurrection of Jesus. The Bride of Christ has become a living temple—a people inhabited by the Holy Spirit who are commissioned to tell God's Story in their services of worship and show His Story by their worship service. The restoration of broken worship now involves the creation and empowering of "lead worshipers," who will offer worship service in every sphere of society and culture.

3. Meditate on the Future Plan for Worship

Every aspect of the new heaven and new earth will perfectly reflect the glory of God and will serve His eternal purposes and pleasure. The new heaven and new earth will be filled with "lead worshipers" who do all things to the glory of God for the pleasure of God, as they offer ceaseless praise through worship service.

IN WHAT WAYS IS WORSHIP BROKEN?

Man's glory has replaced God's glory as the heart of worship. The first worship war was fought by Cain and Abel, and it resulted in murder (Genesis 4). Man's pleasure has taken precedent over God's pleasure as the goal of worship. Think about it. Are there any legitimate grounds for our using phrases such as, "I really liked the worship today," or, "I'm going to find a church that gives me the kind of worship I'm looking for"?

Nothing in creation reflects God's glory as clearly as it once did. Life has been compartmentalized into the sacred and the secular (work vs. worship, worship leaders vs. lead worshipers). Services of worship have also been compartmentalized into the "worship" part of the service (usually the music) and the rest of the service. If hearing and responding to the Word of God is not an act of worship for us, then God have mercy.

The worship of the creature (man) and created things (idolatry) has replaced the worship of the Creator (Romans 1:21–25). Worshiping worship has replaced worshiping God. To worship God is to be preeminently concerned to bring Him pleasure and honor. To worship is to be primarily concerned with our pleasure and satisfaction. If we happen to enjoy services of worship, great! The truth is we should; for what should bring us greater delight than to pleasure the heart of God? But our enjoyment is not the goal; it's simply a gift.

For Personal and Community Reflection

Are you a "true worshiper" or someone who simply likes "great worship"?

Is it God you worship or the experience of worship that you worship? How can you know the difference? When it comes to worship, do you have a consuming passion (a need to be fulfilled) or one consummate passion (a commitment to be poured out for the glory of Jesus)? Has worship become merely the musical/liturgical equivalent of your favorite ice cream, cut of meat, or Starbuck's coffee?

What are your particular "broken cisterns," your idols—the things and people that you rely upon for life, fulfillment, and salvation? Your wallet? Boyfriend? Children? Computer? Refrigerator? Self-righteousness? Wounds? Ministry? Athletic prowess? Parents' approval? Sexual addiction? Drugs?

Come to Jesus today, like the Samaritan woman and those who believed her story. Where else is there to go? "The Spirit and the Bride say, 'Come.' And let the one who hears say, 'Come.' And let the one who is thirsty come; let the one who desires take the water of life without price" (Revelation 22:17).

LEARNING TO WORSHIP *Now* AS WE SHALL WORSHIP *Then*

Revelation 21:1–22:5 gives us a vision of the perfected worship we shall experience for eternity. You can forget any notions of being bored with floating around while strumming a harp and singing endless rounds of "Kumbayah." Check out just some of the aspects revealed about the New Jerusalem:

1. The new heaven and new earth—the new-creation world of shalom and righteousness (21:1).

2. A city whose entire population is radiant with the joy and fascination of a just-married bride (21:2).

3. A city alive with perfected relationships and redeemed stories (21:3–8).

4. A city of consummate beauty, architectural wonder, and fulfilled promises (21:9–21).

5. A city whose temple is God and whose light is the glory of the Lamb of God (21:22–23).

6. A city of pan-national diversity, trans-generational culture, and poly-medium art (21:24–26).

7. A city of inviolate harmony and eternal wholeness (21:27).

8. A garden-city of dynamic life and endless delights (22:1–2).

9. A city liberated for worship service and perfect intimacy with the triune God (22:3–5a).

10. A city whose citizens will exercise dominion and create *new* culture to the glory of God (22:5b).

Combining the Future with the Now

Now knowing the distinction, how can we help our congregations connect *services of worship* with *worship service*? Or better yet, how can we strive toward establishing God's *future worship* through His *present worship*? Here are a few ways:

- Ask your pastor about the possibility of developing a church-wide study on the theme of worship, perhaps creating a ten-to twelve-week series of sermons on such topics as "Giving Our God What He Is Worth: Reflecting on Our Story as a Worshiping Community." Such a series should be accompanied by well-written questions and exercises to be used in Sunday school classes or in your small-group structure.

- Build services of worship that show and tell the history of redemption.

- Encourage your pastors and worship leaders to begin incorporating the language of *worship service* and *services of worship* into the church's vocabulary. This will take a long time, but the investment will be worth the effort. "Bust" anyone who wants to perpetuate using the word *worship* only in reference to the musical portion of a service of worship!

- Don't let your congregation separate its doxological calling from its missional calling. John Piper said it well: "Missions exists because worship does not."

- Regularly (not just during a missions conference!) incorporate songs and musical instruments into your services of worship from the nations and people groups your church family supports. This will help connect your church family with God's larger Story.

- Discover what would be "music in God's ears" in your immediate community, county, city, etc. In other words, where does the transforming and healing power of the gospel need to be manifest around you?

- Allow the *heart of worship service* to shape *the art of your services of worship*. That is, be intentional, not pragmatic when it comes to the worship of God. Concentrate on being faithful, not successful, when it comes to the worship of God.

10 RESTORING GOD'S BROKEN CHURCH

"I saw the holy city, new Jerusalem, coming down out of heaven from
God, prepared as a bride adorned for her husband."
—REVELATION 21:2

"Let Your kingdom come in me, let Your will be done in me
Here on earth as it is and as it will be in Heaven
Show Your glory to the world, tell Your story to the world
Let my life be a preview of coming attractions"
— SCC, "Coming Attractions"

(SCOTTY):

If it's true that he who laughs last laughs the loudest, then prepare to cover your ears. A day is coming when the auditory overloading laughter of God is going to erupt—the day when God connects all the dots of our stories to His. The consummate Story teller will bring all stories to consummation in the world of no more "knowing in part" (1 Corinthians 13:9–10). Great will be our joy, and greater still, will be His.

I'm betting the most repeated phrase we'll hear for the first thousand years in the timeless world of eternity will be, "Oooohhhh, so *that's* what you were up to . . . now I get it!" Many of the things we will experience in this life that make absolutely no sense to us, and even the things that violate our sensibilities, will prove to be the megaphone of God's mercy and the floodlight of His faithfulness.

Debilitating "thorns in the flesh" (2 Corinthians 12:7–10) will become lush, aromatic gardens by the One who makes all things new. Painful and aggravating limitations will be revealed as the conduits through which God's limitless compassion flowed to others. Callings and circumstances that highlighted our weakness will be honored as the billboards which advertised God's greatness. I begin this chapter with such great hope for several reasons.

THE STORIES WE WOULD HAVE NEVER CHOSEN

As I sat at my favorite writing station preparing to write this chapter, I was enthralled and smitten with John's description of the perfected Bride of Christ: beautiful, healed, whole, and so very, very alive. And then it hit me: I've been a pastor in four different decades and in two different centuries. Me! The guy who never dreamt about nor desired, but actually *dreaded,* the thought of working in a church. It's laughable.

In the fall of 1968, if someone had told me one day I would be a pastor, I would have said, "There's a greater chance that I would sing a duet with Paul McCartney at a Super Bowl halftime show." The truth is, if I wasn't convinced God had called me to be a servant to the broken Bride of Jesus, then I would have chosen a much different vocation. For pastoring is often like a dripping spigot—an unremitting irritant that incessantly confronts me with my limits, insufficiency, and idols. And who among us willingly chooses a life story which, by its very nature, will be a narration of our weaknesses? No one does, because it incessantly demands a Savior much bigger than us. That's why God *calls* us to places, like a sheriff delivering a subpoena, and doesn't merely *suggest* a list of possibilities, like a travel agent.

Along with having to laugh at the outworking of God's unlikely plan for my life, I'm also compelled to worship as a result of His magnificent plot for the church. The contrast between the broken church of today and the beautiful church of forever is simply staggering. We're not talking about an ugly duckling becoming a swan, but a prostitute becoming Jesus' queen. And it's this very contrast we must ever keep before us. Individually and corporately, we, the inglorious ones, shall be a cherished and beautiful Bride, aglow with the very glory of God.

Owning our present brokenness will intensify our longings for our coming beauty. But, at the same time, seeing our coming beauty is essential to owning our present brokenness. This is why it's both thrilling and threatening to fill our hearts as full as possible with John's vision of our future as the Bride of Jesus. In one of his earlier letters, John wrote, "Beloved, we are God's children now, and what we will be has not yet appeared; but we know that when he appears we shall be like him, because we shall see him as he is. And everyone who thus hopes in him purifies himself as he is pure" (1 John 3:2–3). Knowing we will be completely like Jesus one day is thrilling and certainly produces hope.

And yet this same promise of Christlikeness is also threatening, not in a way that causes fear, but in that it calls for change. For just as God's ways are not our ways, so God's definition of beauty is *significantly* different from ours. The Bride Jesus is preparing for Himself is not always the one we instinctively choose to become. I know this well, for my spiritual autobiography can be told as a journey between two very different bridal catalogues—two contrasting views of what it means to be the church.

OWNING OUR BROKEN CHURCH STORIES

My "bridal story" begins with the unfortunate saga of having to leave the church of my youth to discover the main song God gave her to sing: the gospel. Like many churches below the Mason-Dixon line, mine was lethally nice. Good people gathering each week to preserve the fabric and faith of our southern culture and community, without giving *any* noticeable evidence of our actually *needing* Jesus and His saving grace.

I came to Christ as a senior in high school through the film ministry of The Billy Graham Association. And, like any new believer, I experienced great joy and peace. But I also had to deal with the sad reality that for the twelve years I was a member of my church, I never heard anyone speak of the Christian life in terms of a personal relationship with Jesus, or even knowing God as a loving Father through the riches of His grace.

When I discovered new life in Christ outside of my church, I felt like I had been deceived and cheated. I left that church with the same disgusted attitude somebody leaves a restaurant with after experiencing incompetent service. It took years to overcome the disillusionment and anger I felt toward the institution of church for failing me.

Decades later, however, I find no joy in remembering the way I reacted to my church as a young believer. Though I can't explain it, I can neither excuse nor justify the arrogance and cynicism I demonstrated. It was so unloving to depersonalize the membership of my home church by labeling them "the institutional church." It wasn't as though they were engaged in a conspiracy to withhold the life-giving grace of Jesus from me. We can only share with one another what we have in our own cupboards. Granted, their cupboard lacked a few vital things; but they were simply as clueless as I was about gospel nutrition.

The members of my home church were dear people with names, faces, and stories, many of whom loved me every way they knew how—especially when my mom was killed in her car wreck. They offered hugs, meals, and invitations for sleepovers; they checked in on me and were sensitive about my first couple of Mother's Days and Christmases without Mom.

Remembering with sadness the degree of cynicism I carried for so long has caused me to take a close look at the growing cynicism the current and emerging generation in America has about church. What's really fueling and driving it? Righteous concern, self-absorbed pouting—or both? It has also caused me to ponder and grieve a fraternal twin of cynicism toward the church, a sibling that currently seems to be on steroids: *consumerism in the church*.

Never have I witnessed a time when evangelical (conservative) Christians have appeared to be more preoccupied with *their* druthers and demands for the church, and yet less concerned with *Jesus'* design and delights for His Bride. In the greater Nashville area, we have more churches per capita than any city in the world. Options, baby, options! Not only can we say, "If you don't like the weather, wait fifteen minutes and it will change," but we can also say, "If you don't like your church in fifteen minutes, you can change." (That is, to another church, of course.) I've lived in this community for the past quarter of a century, and it is not unusual for me to meet individuals who have been members of four or five different churches during that time.

But I cannot be self-righteously critical of either of these diseases, because I am a carrier of both. I realize more than ever, apart from God's grace, I am just as likely to treat marriage to Jesus like I am tempted to treat marriage to Darlene—*selfishly*. "What's in this relationship for me? How can I get more fulfillment and satisfaction?" That's why writing this chapter on the church is painfully wonderful.

The pain comes from having to heal the past and confront present issues, as both participant and pastor in the broken bridal community. But the wonder (which *far* exceeds the pain) comes from being confronted, again and again and again, with the relentless ways Jesus loves us, His fickle and faithless, yet betrothed Bride.

Little Country Church for *Me*

The first positive thought I remember having about church was planted by the band Love Song, who are pioneers of contemporary Christian music. Their song "Little Country Church" tells the story of a small church in Southern California experiencing a fresh visitation of the Holy Spirit. The result of God's powerful presence was a smorgasbord of people being drawn together to share new life and freedom in Jesus. Everything in the church got turned upside-down! I loved the imagery: "Long hairs, short hairs, some coats and ties / People came from miles around."

As a new believer in the spring of '68, this story of revival on the West Coast sounded so very cool and revolutionary to me—and completely foreign to anything I'd ever experienced. And like ripples emanating from a big splash on a placid pond, the effects of the California-based Jesus Movement (in the mid-'60s and early '70s) were beginning to show up in North Carolina. Guitars and drums began to make their presence known in our sanctuaries as well. Jeans and flannel shirts weren't just worn to off-campus youth group meetings, but on Sunday mornings. We were breaking out of bondage, coming forth from the Egypt of dead religion and ecclesiastical slavery! Our not-so-silent cry became, "Down with the traditions of man . . . up with the freedom of the Spirit!" Freedom to sing choruses and not just hymns. Freedom to replace the pulpit with an overhead projector and lectern. Freedom to lift our hands in worship and not just fold them politely. Freedom to use Fritos and Pepsi as communion wine and bread, if need be. Freedom from church programs and organization. Freedom to sit on the floor and not just in pews.

Looking back, what we called "freedom" seems pathetically tame and pitifully self-absorbed, especially as I look ahead to the Bride we are becoming. Nonetheless, the alluring image of a "little country church" in revival got burned in my heart. Unfortunately, this alluring image started to function more like a graven image. I began tearing down the "graceless church" of my youth as a part of my testimony. And I unwittingly began sketching architectural plans for an equally graceless church—one with important foundational elements, but with a self-serving superstructure and lots of personally satisfying curb appeal.

Over the course of time, my "little country church" mutated and morphed into several other forms as my taste buds and theological nuance changed. Among the most self-indulgent was the "little Alpine church in South Central Switzerland"—comprised of fifty good, self-sufficient friends, all enjoying the same music, liturgy, authors, theology, food, and relational style. If this sounds more like a college fraternity or an elitist fly-fishing club than a local church, you've discerned well. How did my cynical reaction to my home church make it so easy for me to slip into an ecclesiastical consumerism mode?

Follow my reasoning: "My church didn't give me the gospel. It's right for me to expect a church to present the good news of Jesus and His grace—that's their main business. Hmmm, I wonder what else they didn't give me. Let's see . . . discipleship, Bible study, classes on topics that interest me, the new contemporary music I'm connecting with. OK, I'm out of here. I'll look till I find a church that will give me everything I need and have a right to expect."

CROSSING THE LINE FROM CONCERN TO CONSUMERISM

The problem with my reasoning wasn't with the issues I raised, but with the direction I took. We *must* be concerned for the foundational elements—the "means of grace"—that Jesus declares essential for *every* church. To name a few: the inspiration and authority of the Bible, Christ-centered worship, good teaching and gospel preaching, prayer, fellowship, discipleship, the sacraments of baptism and the Lord's Supper. All of these are very important gifts that God provides to help us grow into spiritual maturity and to equip us for service. But oh, how easily we can turn *any* of God's good gifts—including grace itself—into a means of seeking our own pleasure and fulfillment. Consider these two scenarios:

A young man received a full scholarship all the way through Johns Hopkins Medical School, and then was given the internship and residency other students dreamed about. However, after completing his free education and wonderful training, he never practiced medicine a single day of his life. Instead, he just hung out at Starbucks, discussing the failures of the American health care system and living off an inheritance he received from his father's estate.

A young woman went on a summer missions trip to Haiti, the summer before she began college. While in Port au Prince, she became greatly convicted about the plight of the poor—especially how hunger is exacerbated in Haiti because of the horrible growing conditions, as most trees are cut down for heating and cooking purposes, which leads to massive erosion problems. Choosing to be a part of the solution, she majored in agronomy, with a special emphasis on drip irrigation systems and issues of reforestation for countries like Haiti. After graduating with honors, however, she never returned to Haiti. She married a successful investment consultant and now uses her training to tend her three-acre, backyard wildflower garden and a small greenhouse in which she raises orchids.

Here's how my story connects with these two scenarios. During my four years at the University of North Carolina, I was involved in three different campus ministries—simultaneously! Why? Because not one of them met all of *my* needs. For fellowship and friends, I went to Campus Crusade; for solid teaching, I went to InterVarsity;

and for discipleship training, I went to the Navigators. It was as though I turned the Christian life into a big progressive dinner, and I maintained authority over the menu. But good nutrition is no guarantee of good fruition. With all the meetings I was going to, I had little time left over to be with nonbelievers, or to engage in any form of mercy ministry, or even for building significant relationships with friends.

For the first seven years after I became a Christian, I refused to join or even participate in a church. I simply couldn't find one that met *my* standards. I left a church that didn't take care of me, and I couldn't find one good enough for me. An old cliché says, "The reason they call it 'sin' is because 'I' is right in the middle of it." Though a zealous believer, I was living solely for me.

I took God's good gifts in a direction they were never meant to be taken. I crossed over from the zone of a healthy concern for spiritual disciplines into the land of self-serving consumerism. The apostle Paul encountered an ugly version of this same problem in the church at Corinth. "Your meetings do more harm than good. . . . When you come together, it is not the Lord's Supper you eat, for as you eat, each of you goes ahead without waiting for anybody else. One remains hungry, another gets drunk. . . . Do you despise the church of God and humiliate those who have nothing?" (1 Corinthians 11:17, 20–22 NIV).

Have you ever been at a covered-dish meal with a group of kids? They rush to be first in line and then try to out-grab one another for the biggest chicken breast on the table, for the biggest piece of cake, and for the cookies with the most M&M's in them. Something similar was going on in Corinth. Believers were abusing the "Agape Meal"— an early church version of a covered-dish supper that included the celebration of the Lord's Supper. The very meal that brings believers to Jesus' Cross of self-denial was being used as a meal of self-fulfillment. The net result? The poor remained hungry, believers got drunk on communion wine, and the church was despised.

There are a variety of ways this same self-indulgent attitude can be manifest. Consider the following descriptions of contemporary church models. Do any of these slight parodies look familiar? Is your heart reflected in one or more of these?

A Private Club in the Suburbs — A gathering for busy, "successful" Christians looking for good teaching and happy, safe kids; familiar faces; and reasonable dues.

A Retreat Center in the Rockies — A furnace for spiritual experience and dynamic inspiration without the messiness of committed relationships and the costliness of "missional" living.

A Food Court at the Mall — A congregation of upwardly mobile consumers, providing multiple options and exciting offerings to keep everybody happy and coming back. A veritable buffet of possibilities to meet everyone's particular fancy and ever-changing appetites.

A Religious Fort in the Wilderness — A church with high walls, little diversity, many opinions, and few doubts—and with even fewer nonbelievers inquiring about the "hope within." This is full of those who love to confirm their prejudices and harden their categories.

A Spiritual Theater for the Weekends — A gathering of "patrons" of the spiritual arts who love to share critiques with one another of oratory, music, scripts, and performance. A haven for inspiration without transformation, and religious rhetoric without the rigors of community development and cultural investment.

But here's the paradox and the crux of this situation: the richer our experience of God's grace, the less we should be living as consumers and the more we should be living as the consumed ones. We are to be "living sacrifices"—a people, who in response to God's never-ending mercies for us in Jesus, live for *His* glory and the benefit of *others* (Romans 12:1–2), and not to please *ourselves*. "We who are strong ought to bear with the failings of the weak and not to please ourselves. Each of us should please his neighbor for his good, to build him up. For even Christ did not please himself" (Romans 15:1–3 NIV).

What then is the primary indicator that we've crossed the line from healthy concern into self-serving consumerism? If our experience of God's Word, the gospel, worship, fellowship, etc., gets us to the "right" church, but does little to involve us in God's Story, then we've *crashed* the border. If we are giving little, if any, evidence of a missional lifestyle, being a means by which Jesus is bringing restoration to the broken things, then we may have already made application for permanent residency in the land of consumerism. God have mercy on us.

The church is the only "fraternity" in the world designed to have a primary concern for nonmembers and non-"pledges." We are to "rush" the has-beens and the socially lost, to go after the unwashed and unwanted, and to get the marginalized and the oppressed in "our house." Indeed, the "fraternity row" of the gospel should be built in the neighborhoods with poison-ivy-infested yards, not in the gated communities of Ivy League elitism.

If It Ain't Broke, Don't Fix It?

Ironically, the *little country church* that Love Song was singing about went on to become the suburban mega-church of Calvary Chapel in

Costa Mesa, California. Chuck Smith had no way of anticipating the exponential growth in numbers and challenges he would face in the following years. Neither did I.

When five couples felt called to plant a church in downtown Franklin, Tennessee, in the spring of 1986, we envisioned it growing to 500 members, maybe, and then leveling off. Though we had a great purpose statement, a well-defined set of core values, and a healthy philosophy of ministry, we had no idea of how hungry people were for the gospel of God's grace—or what to do with them as they began streaming into Franklin.

Within seven years, five couples became 4,000 people cramming into as many as five services on Sunday. Though Jesus was mightily at work, it became hard to distinguish the difference between the intoxicating thrill of "success" and the joy that the Holy Spirit gives in confirming the pleasure of God. Never having been a senior pastor before, *nothing* could have prepared me for the overwhelming growth we experienced—and all by word of mouth. Seminary doesn't really prepare you for the shift from being an associate pastor to becoming a senior pastor—namely the temptations, hardships, idols, and much more baggage that come with your new "package."

But huge numbers and large offerings have a way of sending a deceiving message that's hard *not* to translate as, "We must be doing *something* right. And as they say, 'If ain't broke, don't fix it.'" Unfortunately, that's a common, but dangerous, conclusion that many churches reach. The truth is, the church *is* "broke"—*comprehensively* broken—just like all pastors. And the clearest evidence of our brokenness is that we seldom realize it.

Jesus confronts churches and Christians who are oblivious to their brokenness with the same words He spoke to the church in Laodicea. "You say, 'I am rich; I have acquired wealth and do not need a thing.' But you do not realize that you are wretched, pitiful, poor, blind and naked. . . . Those whom I love I rebuke and discipline" (Revelation 3:17, 19 NIV). Jesus loves us well when He exposes our true condition. And lately, Jesus has been loving me *really well*.

I'm fortunate enough to have been involved in a charismatic house church of fifteen people (my *little country church* experience), a mainline denomination church in renewal, the explosive growth of my first church plant, the ecstasy and agony of planting daughter churches, and the transition season from being pastor of "the church of the big buzz" to being pastor of a church on the other side of its buzz. I've even had a modicum of the Alpine experience, having taught the Scriptures and worshiped in Switzerland seven times.

But looking back on all of these experiences, I now say, with deep conviction and great joy, that the *only thing* that matters is to discover what Jesus wants, in and from His church—His beloved Bride—and seek to honor His design and delights with everything we have and are.

Personally, we may like the *style* of a little country church, the *ambiance* of a little Alpine church, or the *programs* of the user-friendly church. We may fall in love with the *buzz* of the newest "everybody's-going-there" church, the *worship* of the artsy ancient orthodox church, the *fellowship* of the church-of-no-strangers, the *edge* of the postmodern "show-me-don't-tell-me church" . . . or any of the good things offered in a *multitude* of designer churches. But are we concerned, above *everything* else, to become the Bride Jesus has died to make of us? Our calling isn't to be relevant, effective, or successful churches, but to be the loving and faithful Bride of Jesus.

As we take a closer look at the "bridal catalogue" of the Scriptures, we must prepare ourselves—make that, *brace* ourselves—for some surprises. For Jesus' taste in Brides most definitely contrasts, even collides with ours. Let's take a look.

HERE COMES THE BRIDE

As I studied John's electrifying account of Jesus' wedding day, it didn't take me long to realize that his version of the classic processional song, "Here Comes the Bride," breaks all the rules of literary decorum and bridal imagery. John mixes two metaphors that, on first blush, seem terribly incongruent, if not cringe-worthy. "Everyone rise! Here comes the beautifully dressed Bride of Jesus . . . the Holy *City*!" Say what? Jesus' Bride looks like a *city*? That's kind of like saying, "I'd like you to meet my cute little sister the *shopping center*, and my mother the *mega-mall*."

And yet, a closer look at John's imagery confirms that no bridal boutique in New York, Paris, or London, or any wedding ceremony in the history of nuptials, can boast of a more breathtaking Bride as the one Jesus has secured for Himself. And since Jesus delights in having a Bride whose beauty is that of a *city*, our joy should be in discovering the elements and substance of a *metropolis* that cause *Him* so much joy.

What then *is* the significance of Jesus' Bride appearing as a city? To start with, the fact that she is a "holy" city puts the emphasis where it should be—on the matchless love of her Bridegroom in laying down His life for her (Ephesians 5:25–27). Only Jesus would take such an unlikely Bride and beautify her for himself; and only the God of all grace would joyfully present *this* Bride to His Son. This explains why John *twice* describes her as "coming down out of heaven from God" (Revelation 21:2, 10). We're not meant to envision a Bride descending a spiral staircase during the processional, or the church floating down out of the air on clouds at the end of history. This isn't a picture of *space*, but of *grace*.

Our "coming-down-from-heavenness" underscores the wonder of the gospel. The *only* explanation for this better-than-any-fairytale love story can be found in God Himself. We are married to Jesus through the eternal plan and great mercy of our heavenly Father. We could *never* endear ourselves to Jesus or deserve such a Bridegroom.

CITY INVASION

But what else does this metropolitan metaphor imply? Though the downtown area of a community is *strategic* for planting healthy churches, not every church is mandated to locate within the inner city. The majority of local churches in the first three centuries were house churches spread *throughout* the community—in the business districts, rural areas, and even "on the edge of town."

Though *location* is an extremely important issue, the main issue is *vocation*. Not too long ago, I began to explore the unique characteristics of a *city*, and to consider how *city* is developed as a theme throughout God's Story. Like a gifted physician, Eugene Peterson's reflections helped me tremendously at this point—only, his aid was more like the kind a physician gives you when he accurately diagnoses a disease.

A garden is life blessed and ordered by God. Paradise is a garden in Genesis. Love is a garden in the Song of Songs. But cities are noisy with self-assertion, forgetful and defiant of God, battering and abusive to persons. The first city, Enoch, was built by the first murderer, Cain, and destroyed in the Noachic flood. The second city, Babel, was built in an arrogant attempt to storm heaven and was abandoned in a tangle of broken languages. When St. John gave us his vision of judgment, it was a city that was destroyed: "Fallen, fallen is Babylon the great!" (Revelation 18:2).

Heaven surely should get us as far away from that as possible. Haven't we had enough of cities on earth? Don't we deserve what we long for? Many people want to go to heaven the way they want to go to Florida—they think the weather will be an improvement and the people decent. But the biblical heaven is not a nice environment far removed from the stress of hard city life. It is the invasion of the city by the City.[1]

When I read that last phrase, "the invasion of the city by the City," it was as though the lights went on and an X-ray of my whole "church story" was planted on the bright viewing screen, clearly revealing an ecclesiastical abnormality. So many of my wrong ideas about church life are confronted by the combination of those eight little words.

God never designed the church merely to be a *spiritual component of a city*, in the same way health clubs, businesses, schools, walk-in clinics, art galleries, banks, and courthouses are important components of a city. Neither did he call the church just to be the *moral conscience of the city*.

Rather, the church, in a very unique sense, *is a city*— a covenant community of believers married to Jesus. We are called to reveal *today* a little of the *city-life* we will enjoy with Jesus *forever*. Our Bridegroom has given this charge to the church of every generation.

> You are the light of the world. A city on a hill cannot be hidden. Neither do people light a lamp and put it under a bowl. Instead they put it on its stand, and it gives light to everyone in the house. In the same way, let your light shine before men, that they may see your good deeds and praise your Father in heaven (Matthew 5:14–16 NIV).

The church is "a city set on a hill," not the spiritual thermostat in the city, and not a disengaged retreat center hovering above the city. And, as a *city*, we are to offer a glimmer of the glow of the *coming City*. We are to bring Jesus' light into the dark places of society and His restoring love into every aspect of city life. Our Bridegroom has an interest in every sphere of city life, so as His Bride, shouldn't we?

CANNED ASPARAGUS, BEEF LIVER, AND LUTEFISK

Back to Eugene Peterson's analogy: capital C *City* is shorthand for Jesus' Bride living *every* dimension of life to the glory of God in the new heaven and new earth: lower-case c *city* is shorthand for the church's calling to seek to do *all things* to the glory of God on earth, as we will do them one day in heaven. The *City* invades the *city* as we, in the church, are more fully captured by the truth and grace of the gospel, and live as salt and light throughout our communities.

Like every bride preparing for her wedding day, the Bride of Jesus can be distracted with many things—often the wrong things. So how can John's vision help us focus on that which matters the most to our Bridegroom?

> We enter heaven not by escaping what we don't like, but by the sanctification of the place in which God has placed us. . . . There is not as much as a hint of escapism in St. John's heaven. This is not a long (eternal) weekend away from the responsibilities of employment and citizenship, but the intensification and healing of them. Heaven is formed out of dirty streets and murderous alleys, adulterous bedrooms and corrupt courts, hypocritical synagogues and commercialized churches, thieving tax-collectors and traitorous disciples: a city, but now a holy city.[2]

The church was never commissioned to be a refuge from the messiness of city life, or a fort whose walls are topped with razor wire protecting "us" from "them." Jesus has no intent on establishing a cocoon insulating Christians from the contaminating influences of the urban world. Though He says we are not to be *of* the world, He has commissioned us to be *in* it.

Neither was the church designed to be something liked or not liked, in the same way you either like or don't like canned asparagus, beef liver, or lutefisk. This doesn't imply, for a nanosecond, that our experience of church is to be devoid of passion, pleasure, and joy. Just the opposite! This City is also a Garden, and the pervasive delights of the Garden of Eden were just a preview of what is to come in the

Garden City. The river of life, tree of life, and Lord of life will bring everlasting joy to the City.

> Then the angel showed me the river of the water of life, bright as crystal, flowing from the throne of God and of the Lamb through the middle of the street of the city; also, on either side of the river, the tree of life with its twelve kinds of fruit, yielding its fruit each month. The leaves of the tree were for the healing of the nations (Revelation 22:1–2).

Unfortunately, the joy we usually settle for is just as tame and self-absorbed as the freedom I settled for in my "little country church" days. In reality, the Alpine experience *God* has planned for us makes mine look like a day of staring at a pimple. We are *far* too easily satisfied and *way* too unsuspecting of our condition. Indeed, the *city* needs to be invaded by the *City*, just as a hostage needs to be liberated by a Deliverer. We are captives to small-heartedness, prisoners of self-centeredness, and enslaved to our stinginess.

Let's be honest: do we *really* want to be free to walk with broken people and to enter the broken places of injustice, oppression, poverty, spiritual blindness, dysfunction, and disease all around us? Do we *really* want the joy of bringing the healing power of the City into the hating precincts of Enoch, the arrogant streets of Babel, and the dark neighborhoods of Babylon? Do we honestly want that kind of joy and freedom for ourselves and our churches? Or would a couple of great worship services a month, a warm small-group fellowship, and a safe-haven youth group for the kids suffice? *Surely*, we're better than *that*. *Surely*, we realize we've been made for so much more.

A GLORIOUS MIXED MARRIAGE

John reveals a vision of the ultimate urban renewal—the transformation of the comprehensively broken *city* of man into the consummately beautiful *City* of God. The City Bride emerges from decadence to delight, from dirty streets to streets of gold, from adulterous bedrooms to Jesus' wedding chamber, from thieving tax collectors to unselfish servants, and from commercialized churches to glorified worshipers.

The beloved disciple paints with a brush wet with the vivid colors and rich hues of God's grace in describing Jesus' "rare jewel" of a Bride. Let's follow John.

> "Come, I will show you the Bride, the wife of the Lamb." And he carried me away in the Spirit to a great, high mountain, and showed me the holy city Jerusalem coming down out of heaven from God, having the glory of God, its radiance like a most rare jewel, like a jasper, clear as crystal (Revelation 21:9–11).

Notice that we are both spectators and the spectacle in John's vision; those who are shown the Bride, and the Bride who is revealed. What an honor!

> It had a great, high wall, with twelve gates, and at the gates twelve angels, and on the gates the names of the twelve tribes of the sons of Israel were inscribed—on the east three gates, on the north three gates, on the south three gates, and on the

west three gates. And the wall of the city had twelve foundations, and on them were the twelve names of the twelve
apostles of the Lamb (vv. 12–14).

What a testimony this vision is to God's faithfulness. His
promise, revealed to Abraham, to redeem a pan-national people has
been fulfilled! It is also an encouraging picture of reconciliation and
peace. The City-Bride has twelve gates with the names of the *twelve
tribes of the sons of Israel* written on them, and it has twelve foundations on which the names of the *twelve apostles of the Lamb* are
inscribed. The whole family of God—from Israel and every nation of
the world—is symbolically represented as integral and integrated
elements in the New Jerusalem.

This day will mark the end to all racism, imperialism, ethnic
idolatries, injustice, prejudice, oppression, nationalism, genocide,
war . . . every imaginable hostility between humans. It will also mark
the beginning of the eternal celebration of our pan-national diversity
and inviolate unity. We will love, honor, and serve one another with
consummate intimacy and joy forever.

And the one who spoke with me had a measuring rod of
gold to measure the city and its gates and walls. The city lies
foursquare; its length the same as its width. And he
measured the city with his rod, 12,000 stadia. Its length and
width and height are equal. He also measured its wall, 144
cubits by human measurement, which is also an angel's
measurement. The wall was built of jasper, while the city was
pure gold, clear as glass. The foundations of the wall of the

city were adorned with every kind of jewel. The first was jasper, the second sapphire, the third agate, the fourth emerald, the fifth onyx, the sixth carnelian, the seventh chrysolite, the eighth beryl, the ninth topaz, the tenth chrysoprase, the eleventh jacinth, the twelfth amethyst. And the twelve gates were twelve pearls, each of the gates made of a single pearl, and the street of the city was pure gold, transparent as glass (vv. 15–21).

The use of the "golden measuring rod" suggests these measurements are symbolic, emphasizing the symmetry and harmony of the relationships in the city whose family tree is the Cross of Jesus. The point is to fill our hearts with a vision of the perfection of all relationships, not to figure out how this many people could fit into John's architectural renderings of the ideal cityscape. This isn't to imply that John wants us to think only in "spiritual" terms, as opposed to literal realities. For nothing is more "real" than the new world Jesus is creating. Rather, he is emphasizing that the glory of our future—and all of the elements of life in the new heaven and new earth—transcend human ability to measure such things. It requires a tape measure far different than ours!

The City-Bride is described in terms of the Holy of Holies, the most sacred place inside the temple, in which only Israel's high priest was permitted to enter. Even he could do so only one day of the year—on Yom Kippur, the Day of Atonement. In John's vision, the most holy place measures 3,225,000 cubic miles, compared to its counterpart in the temple, which was a mere 2,700 cubic feet. The life, death, and resurrection of Jesus have secured an eternal life of perfect intimacy for the people of God. In every way, our relationships in the new heaven and new earth will be defined and deluged with the presence of God.

John uses images of beauty to describe our relationships. There is no need to look for a tit-for-tat correlation between a particular stone and a particular people group. This City-Bride is hewn from the quarries of God's broken people of every generation, from people groups before Israel, from Israel, and from all nations. It is constructed from a geological history of unlikely men and women rescued and joined together as living stones through the gospel (1 Peter 2:4ff.) and now set in place as precious gems, as in a high priest's breastplate—to be cherished by the Great High Priest of heaven forever!

TANTALIZING THE CULTURE WITH A TASTE OF THE WORLD TO COME

What then are the implications of our coming wedding day for this present waiting day? We are to give onlookers a glimpse of how the grace of Jesus changes self-centered suburbanites into communities of loving urbanites. We must be the servant-citizens who work in the broken places of the world to bring the firstfruits of the new heaven and new earth; we are the good neighbors who courageously sacrifice to push back the effects of the Fall by the expulsive power of the love of God. So what does this look like?

First, take a look at the old city of Jerusalem. Known as the "City of Peace," it was to be a place of:

- Worship and refuge
- Governance and justice

- Residency and relationships
- Culture and creativity
- Resource and industry
- Education and communication
- Art and beauty

All of these elements of city life will also be a part of our life in the New Jerusalem. They serve as categorical reminders of how we should seek to bring the restoring grace and power of Jesus into every part of our communities today. As churches wanting to live as a "city set on a hill," let us live in God's Story as . . .

A Joyful Proclamation of the Kingdom's Arrival
We are to give concrete and compassionate evidence of the presence of our King and His transforming kingdom. Seek to identify some of the particular broken places and broken people in your community, and show up as a servant people who humbly desire to bring the healing presence of the kingdom of God. Specific issues to address may be: poverty, hunger, housing, the arts, various social and mercy ministries, community development concerns, and public education.

A Transforming Presence in a World of Darkness
What are some of the "strongholds of darkness" in your community in which you can demonstrate the victory of Jesus over Satan and the powers of darkness? What captivities, enslavements, and demonic bondages can be identified and addressed in the love and power of the gospel? Some examples of areas to tackle may be:

racism; addictions of all kinds; abuse issues—sexual, physical, and emotional; domestic violence; witchcraft; and depression.

An Encouraging Preview of Coming Attractions
Think of your local church as a "model home" in an urban redevelopment area. Along this line, here are some questions to ponder in community conversation.

- Are you building bridges or throwing grenades as you encounter a nonbelieving world? How would you know? Give some examples of each of these.
- What are some practical ways you can "beautify the Bride of Jesus"? In other words, how can you help to bring the City into your own city-churches? How does your church family need to change? How can you help?
- How can you make the truth of the gospel more believable, without compromising its truth?

FOR FURTHER REFLECTION

Revelation 2–3 records Jesus' affirmations, rebukes, and instructions for the seven churches of Asia Minor. Although there were more than seven churches in Asia Minor, there are good reasons to believe that these seven, taken together, are given to us as a composite picture of the priorities and passions Jesus intends *every* local church to embrace—seven being a number representing completion, or fullness, in the Bible.

Try taking time as a Sunday school class, or with a small group of friends, to study and meditate through these two chapters in Revelation and each of the seven churches profiled. Make a list of the themes and emphases Jesus stresses in His loving and firm words to each of the seven churches. Ponder the implications of what Jesus teaches you for your local church family, as you seek to understand how to more faithfully live as a little "city set on a hill" in your community. Perhaps you could even encourage your pastor to bring a series of messages to the whole congregation on "What Jesus Thinks of His Church," as based on this part of God's Word. To help get you started, I have included a brief blurb about each of the seven churches. May this spur you on to deeper study and greater faithfulness.

Marks of a Church Following Jesus into Restoration:
- Ephesus — A vibrant love for Jesus and others (2:1–7)
- Smyrna — Faithfulness in suffering (2:8–11)
- Pergamum — Consistency in applying the gospel (2:12–17)
- Thyatira — A commitment to the peace and purity of the Church (2:18–29)
- Sardis — Ongoing renewal and reality (3:1–6)
- Philadelphia — Courageous missional living (3:7–13)
- Laodicea — Repentance, humility, and fellowship centered in Jesus (3:14–22)

11 RESTORING BROKEN CULTURE

"*Genesis 1:26 teaches us that God had a purpose in creating man in His image: namely, that man should have dominion over all living creatures and that he should multiply and spread out over the world, subduing it. If now we comprehend the force of this subduing under the term* culture, *now generally used for it, we can say that* culture *in its broadest sense is the purpose for which God created man after His image.*"
— HERMAN BAVINCK

"*All that is truly good and beautiful in this world will reappear there, purified and enhanced in the perfect setting its Maker intended for it; nothing of real value is lost.*"
—MICHAEL WILCOCK

"*A day is coming when all will be fed*
There won't be a single hungry mouth begging for bread
A day is coming when every disease
Will be swept away as mercy floods through every street"
— SCC, "Coming Attractions"

(SCOTTY):

I never get nearly as jazzed about watching the summer Olympics as I do the winter games. Skiers fearlessly barrel down an icy launching pad, hurl themselves like wingless gliders into mid-air; hockey players combine the skills of ballet dancers, barroom bouncers, and expert marksmen while they sprint on two thin blades of razor-edged steel. *These* are the athletes and events that grab my attention!

And yet *no* scene in *any* Olympiad (including the American hockey team's magical defeat of Russia in 1980!) grabbed my attention and emotions like the closing ceremonies of the Summer Olympics of 2004, held in Athens, Greece, which was the birthing room of the Olympics.

With the games over, the formalities completed, and the Olympic flame extinguished, it was time to party! For at least an hour, I sat motionless and mesmerized, feasting upon the captivating beauty of adult-children at play. The tastefully designed Coliseum became a serving bowl of cultural ambrosia, as a global TV audience of millions watched thousands of the earth's most skilled sportsmen intermingle. The athletes were embracing one another with open arms—trading uniform parts, high-fives, and addresses, relishing new friendships and photo ops—treasuring a *brief* moment devoid of all barriers and bravado.

Only two weeks earlier, these disciplined athletes, representing the nations of the world, marched regimentally into the Coliseum, preparing to do battle with one another. Now, however, the playing field of hard-fought competition became a playground of international celebration. Combatants were now comrades, laughs replaced laps, and dueling gave way to dancing.

I've never witnessed as many cultures represented in one place with disarming smiles, virtually on every single face. If only one general session of the United Nations could be filled with as much joy and good will. In a post-9/11, present Iraqi-war world, this image of a great family reunion was truly special and worth savoring.

CULTURE FEST

The timing of this visual smorgasbord could not have been better. For it brought to life an intriguing but perplexing scene in John's vision of the new heaven and new earth that I'd been meditating on for quite a while. The apostle describes an international gathering—similar to the Olympics in pageantry and excitement—in which the kings of the earth stream into the New Jerusalem, which is aglow with the magnetic brightness of God's glory. As they come, they bring the *splendor*, *glory*, and *honor*—the cultural artifacts and treasures—of the nations with them.

> The nations will walk by its light, and the kings of the earth will bring their splendor into it. On no day will its gates ever be shut, for there will be no night there. The glory and honor of the nations will be brought into it. Nothing impure will ever enter it, nor will anyone who does what is shameful or deceitful, but only those whose names are written in the Lamb's book of life (Revelation 21:24–27 NIV).

So what does John's culture-fest of a party signify? Who are these kings, and what stuff of *this* world could God possibly want to be brought into the next? Most of my life, as a believer, I've been told, "It's all going to burn," and, "The only things that are going to last from this world into the next are the *Word of God* and the *people of God*." So what in this world (and in the next) did John intend us to understand by this picture? These were some of the questions and issues I wrestled with as I began studying this passage.

I discovered that John borrowed images from the prophet Isaiah in this passage, not as a plagiarist, but as a participant in the fulfillment of extraordinary promises God made through the prophet seven centuries earlier. The Spirit of God enabled Isaiah to see many of the inconceivable wonders of the Messianic age from afar. John was privileged to get a much closer view—even experiencing the extraordinary world that Isaiah previewed.

Painting with a broad brush, dripping with all the colors of the rainbow, Isaiah presented the work of the Messiah in terms of a great homecoming—that is, a *great home . . . coming to* us! *Nowhere* does the Bible suggest the reason God sent Jesus into this world was to fill up heaven with redeemed souls. Rather, God sent Jesus, ultimately, to bring the fullness of heaven *to us*—to "fill up" every broken place of His cosmos with His grace and glory.

OUR COMING HOME

To understand this part of John's vision, I spent a season meditating on the portions of Isaiah that fueled the apostle's imagination. I was equally taken with both Isaiah's message and his *manner*. He's like a parent having to do the unthinkable: wake up his children on Christmas morning to get them to come downstairs and enjoy a mountain of good gifts freely given to them. Unfortunately, Isaiah's audience was deep in the slumberland of spiritual lethargy and indifference.

His prophecy also reminded me of remodeling shows, such as *Extreme Makeover: Home Edition* or *Debbie Travis' Facelift*, in which creative designers apply their panache and passion to transform parts of older homes for unsuspecting owners—at no cost! (I keep waiting for my phone to ring.) The highlight of these programs is watching the expressions of astonishment and joy that light up the faces of the homeowners when they get a glimpse of their recreated living space.

For Isaiah, the living space is a *whole city*: Jerusalem. In fact, he envisioned a day of *ultimate* cultural transformation of the old City. Just *how* ultimate of a transformation? Well, if you combine all the Olympiads and all the great art galleries and gardens of the world . . . gather the complete riches of music, inventiveness, writing, science, film, economics, craftsmanship, technology, leadership, engineering, and architecture from throughout the history of mankind . . . then you can begin to imagine the world Isaiah and John dare us to believe is coming and all because of the person and work of Jesus.

Indeed, to take Isaiah and John seriously is to realize that the culture of the New Jerusalem will *far* exceed the combined splendor of all the great cultures that have *ever* existed, inclusive of the Garden of Eden. Take a look at Isaiah's words:

Get out of bed, Jerusalem! Wake up. Put your face in the sunlight. GOD's bright glory has risen for you. The whole earth is wrapped in darkness, all people sunk in deep darkness, but GOD rises on you, His sunrise glory breaks over you. Nations will come to your light, kings to your sunburst brightness.

Look up! Look around! Watch as they gather, watch as they approach you; your sons coming from great distances, your daughters carried by their nannies. When you see them coming you'll smile—big smiles! Your heart will swell and, yes, burst! All those people returning by sea for the reunion, a rich harvest of exiles gathered in from the nations!

And then streams of camel caravans as far as the eye can see, young camels of nomads in Midian and Ephah, pouring in from the south from Sheba, loaded with gold and frankincense, preaching the praises of GOD. And yes, a great roundup of flocks from the nomads in Kedar and Nebaioth, welcome gifts for worship at my altar as I bathe my glorious Temple in splendor.

What's that we see in the distance, a cloud on the horizon, like doves darkening the sky? It's ships from the distant islands, the famous Tarshish ships returning your children from faraway places, loaded with riches, with silver and gold, and backed by the name of your GOD, The Holy of Israel, showering you with splendor.

Foreigners will rebuild your walls, and their kings assist you in the conduct of worship. When I was angry I hit you hard. It's my desire now to be tender. Your Jerusalem gates will always be open—open house day and night!—receiving deliveries of wealth from all nations, and their kings, the delivery boys . . .

When you suck the milk of nations and the breasts of royalty, you'll know that I, GOD, am your Savior, your Redeemer, Champion of Jacob. I'll only give you the best—no more hand-me-downs!—Gold instead of bronze, silver instead of iron, bronze instead of wood, iron instead of stones. I'll install Peace to run your country, make Righteousness your boss. There'll be no more stories of crime in your land, no more robberies, no more vandalism. You'll name your main street Salvation Way, and install Praise Park at the center of town.

You'll have no more need of the sun by day nor the brightness of the moon at night. GOD will be your eternal light, your God will bathe you in splendor, your sun will never go down, your moon will never fade. I will be your eternal light.

Your days of grieving are over. All your people will live right and well, in permanent possession of the land. They're the green shoot that I planted, planted with my own hands to display my glory. The runt will become a great tribe, the weakling will become a strong nation. I am GOD. At the right time I'll make it happen (Isaiah 60:1–11, 16–22, MSG).

If you're out of breath and brain cells just from reading Isaiah's master plan, let's break the passage down a little bit. I found it helpful to identify elements of the New Jerusalem highlighted by both Isaiah and John. They tell us the transformed City will perpetually celebrate the welcoming heart of God and the inviolate safety of the City for all, for its twelve gates will never be shut (Isaiah 60:11; Revelation 21:25). The light of God's glory will illuminate the City, eliminating the need for either the sun or moon. Never again will the annoying buzz of a fluorescent light be heard (Isaiah 60:19–20; Revelation 21:23).

Human suffering, in every form, will be eradicated forever, along with all grieving (Isaiah 60:18; Revelation 21:4). The people and kings of the nations will be magnetically drawn to the glory of God permeating the City, and they will enjoy community and conversation by the light of its glow (Isaiah 60:1–3; Revelation 21:24). And there will be a magnificent ingathering of goods, treasures, and artifacts from all the nations of the earth (Isaiah 60:6–7, 9, 13; Revelation 21:24–25).

It's important to notice that while Isaiah depicts the City's kings as captives being led in a victory procession into the City (Isaiah 60:3–5, 11), John describes them freely entering New Jerusalem as equal citizens and cultural participants (Revelation 21:24–26). This isn't a contradiction but a confirmation of the unfolding nature and beauty of God's Story.

The shadows of the Old Testament are fulfilled by the substance of the New Testament. Isaiah wasn't privileged to see the work of Jesus or the wonders of the New Jerusalem like John saw. But *no one*—including God's sons and daughters presently in heaven—has seen the fullness of our coming home, as it will be revealed when Jesus returns to consummate God's Story. The glow of the coming City is dim to all of us, but distinct enough to have its intended impact.

Imagine Isaiah's original audience on the day he first delivered this prophecy. Picture the cameras panning to the faces of the citizens of the *Old* Jerusalem as they tried to envision God's blueprint and relief drawing of the *New* Jerusalem. Here's my *loose* summary/paraphrase of the heart of Isaiah's message: "Wake up from your faithless siestas and your spiritual amnesia, sons and daughters of God! At the appointed time, the God of all grace is going to expand the borders of the old City and fill up a *New* Jerusalem with the everlasting delights of a pan-national, trans-generational, poly-medium cultural life beyond *anything* you've ever dreamed of or would ever ask for!"

How could Isaiah's audience *possibly* absorb or understand a hope with these propositions and proportions? On a much, much smaller scale, it would be like God promising to change Steven's hometown of Paducah, Kentucky, into Paris, France, or my hometown of Graham, North Carolina, into London, England. How seemingly preposterous, unsettling, and thrilling, all at the same time! Indeed, God never planned just to remodel Jerusalem's kitchen, but also her culture and cosmos.

A weary Isaiah was energized by this vision, and an aging John fell on his face in adoration simply beholding it. This same vision brought courage to believers in the face of Roman persecution, and dreams and determination to the fathers of the Reformation. May it grip our hearts and hands as well. What might this look like?

What Is Culture, Anyway?

I've purposefully waited until now to deal with the most obvious question raised by a chapter titled, "Restoring Broken Culture." "What *is* culture?" I've been writing as though we're all on the same definition-of culture-page . . . using phrases like "cultural ambrosia," "culture-fest," "cultural artifacts," and my favorite, "pan-national, trans-generational, poly-medium cultural life."

But how do the Scriptures define the meaning of *culture?* Is it with hoity-toity flare, high-brow snobbery, the raised chin, and heightened suspicions of elitism . . . or the bacterial growth in the bottom of a petri dish? Neither in Isaiah's or John's visions! In essence, *culture* is *creational stewardship in community*. Let's explore the background to this working definition.

The first reference to "culture-making" in the Bible is found in Genesis 1:28, which is often referred to as the "cultural mandate:" "And God blessed them. And God said to them, 'Be fruitful and multiply and fill the earth and subdue it and have dominion over the fish of the sea and over the birds of the heavens and over every living thing that moves on the earth.'"

Indeed, the story of culture-making begins in the Bible like a magnificent musical, with a score, script, choreography, rhythms, and orchestrations for *all* of mankind, creation, and history. All things God made were *good*, and He arranged each of them within a matrix of archetypal beauty, perfect alignment (*shalom*, or righteousness), and synergistic wonder.

In this magnificent cosmos ("beautiful ornament"), God commissioned Adam and Eve and their offspring to *make* culture. They were to work and keep the garden-paradise in which God placed them, and they were to rule and fill the whole earth. Thus, Adam and Eve were given a local vocation with worldwide implications. Culture-making can be understood, therefore, as the sum of these four tasks:

Ruling — Exercising benevolent governance in God's world

Filling — Bringing pervasive expansion of God's glory

Working — Releasing latent potential in God's creation

Keeping — Providing caring stewardship of God's gifts[1]

Adam and Eve were never meant to treat the Garden of Eden as a private retreat center or a gated community protecting them from the rest of God's created universe. In a profound sense, their paradise was to be the paradigm by which they and their posterity would rule, fill, work, and keep the entire earth to the glory and delight of God.

This is why it is imperative for followers of Jesus to become thoroughly versed and immersed in the first two and the last two chapters of the Bible. For God's Story with us begins in a garden (the Garden of Eden) and ends in a global garden-city (the New Jerusalem).

Adam and Eve were called to take the raw and wonderful elements of God's creation, develop their potential, and fill the entire earth with His glory and joy. They were to transform the untamed and untapped resources of nature into a social environment that would reveal the glory of God.

What a magnificent story in which to live! What an unparalleled life calling, which we should simply call *worship service*. Like Adam and Eve, we are to declare God's glory and experience His joy as we take the "Play-Doh" and "Erector Set" of the Garden of Eden and build the global New Jerusalem.

DIGNITY, DEPENDENCE, AND DELIGHT

These are the three words that come to mind when I consider the *cultural mandate* God gave us. What *great dignity* is this calling

219

conferred upon mankind—that God would entrust to His image bearers such privilege and responsibility. Indeed, what is man that God would crown us with such glory and honor? And what a life of *utter dependence* is this mandate commissioned.

Think about it. Who, but God alone, could enable His sons and daughters to fill the earth with His glory? That's like expecting a butterfly to create a new fleet of 747 jets; or a six-year-old batboy to serve as the commissioner of Major League Baseball; or a little girl with three months of Suzuki violin lessons under her belt to write a symphony in a week and take the job as the permanent conductor of the London Philharmonic Orchestra.

And lastly, what supreme and *exquisite delight* is revealed in the cultural mandate. God could have placed Adam and Eve in an expansive open field of swaying grain, on top of a great snow-kissed mountain, or on the sugar-white sandy shore of a roaring ocean. Instead, he placed them in a garden paradise where the sensate pleasures, the aesthetic wonder, and the life-generating nature of nature would fuel their culture-making imaginations with a passion for the good, the true, and the beautiful.

Indeed, how brilliant of God to inaugurate the cultural mandate in a garden, for agriculture was the perfect nursery for generating other dimensions of our culturative calling. In fact, the Latin word for culture, *cultura*, literally means "tillage," implying that culture is the process of tilling and cultivation.

Adam and Eve were to release the hidden potential of the earth through tilling, planting, tending, harvesting, preparing the fruit, enjoying the fruit of their work, and praising God from whom all blessings flow. This cycle would naturally lead to the development and expansion of many other aspects, avenues, and artifacts of cultural advancement in areas such as relationships, governance, ethics, technology, economics, art, and education.

This doxological partnership between God and mankind for the expansion of a garden into a global garden-city would require the combination of multiple skills and the collaboration of many hearts. Strong families and healthy communities (little cities) would need to be formed, so the different gifts and abilities God gave His image bearers could be developed, orchestrated, and liberated for the fruition of our worldwide commission. What a glorious plan!

FILLING OUR STOMACHS OR GOD'S EARTH?

BUT ... Adam and Eve's act of unbelief and rebellion in the Garden of Eden changed *everything*. Sin invaded the hearts of God's creatures and permeated every sphere of God's creation. Instead of filling creation with God's glory, man's glory became filling his own belly. The apostle Paul lamented, "Their god is their stomach, and their glory is in their shame" (Philippians 3:19 NIV). The pleasure of worship was displaced with the worship of pleasure. Men became "lovers of pleasure rather than lovers of God" (2 Timothy 3:4).

Instead of cultivating God's garden, men began exploiting His creation. Humble dominion became selfish domination. Ruling as servants *under* the Lord was replaced with ruling *over* people as self-appointed lords. The "keeping" of stewardship disintegrated into the hoarding of ownership. Instead of building the global New Jerusalem, men began building the godless city of Babylon.

But God did not abandon His creatures, creation, or His decree for culture making. He promised—through the work of the Messiah—to break the curse of sin and death, reconcile His fallen children, restore His broken creation, and to redeem the fractured history of culture making. Indeed, the "filling" of all things is still *the number one item* on God's agenda, because it includes the completion of the Great Commission as well. For the fulfillment of the Great Commission is nothing more, and nothing less, than the gathering of the trans-generational, pan-national family of God into the New Jerusalem. It's culture making in the global city of the new heaven and new earth to the glory of God in the joy of God!

Everything Isaiah and John envisioned will come to pass! Though the first Adam failed miserably in his culturative calling, the Second Adam will succeed majestically.

Jesus died to save sinners—but He is also the Lamb who serves as the lamp in the transformed City. As the Lamb of God, He draws all of the goods, artifacts, and instruments of culture to Himself; the kings of the earth will return their authority and power to the Lamb who sits upon the throne; Jesus is the one whose blood has purchased a multi-national community, composed of people from every tribe and tongue and nation. His redemptive ministry, as the ministry of the Lamb is cosmic in scope. . . .

The God who declares here and now that it is "well" with my soul is the same creating Lord who once looked at the whole world which He had made and proclaimed, "This is good!" This God wants once again to say that things are "well" with His entire creation—and He will someday do so when He announces, "Behold, I make all things new. . . . It is done! I am the Alpha and the Omega, the Beginning and the End" (Revelation 21:5–6 NKJV). "It is well with my soul" is only a first step, an initial fruit of God's redeeming activity. We must share in God's restless yearning for the renewal of the cosmos. . . .

Our conviction—our sure hope—that the Lord will bring these things to pass in His own time should lead us to express our discipleship boldly. Our present efforts as citizens of Zion will culminate in the final victory of the Lamb whose light will fill the city.[2]

How can we fuel our "restless yearning for the renewal of the cosmos"? One of the ways is to meditate continually on the cultural life we will enjoy in the New Jerusalem, as revealed in the Scriptures. What has Jesus purchased and promised to us? Let's take a closer look at John's vision.

The nations will walk by its light, and the kings of the earth will bring their splendor into it. On no day will its gates ever be shut, for there will be no night there. The glory and honor of the nations will be brought into it. Nothing impure will ever enter it, nor will anyone who does what is shameful or deceitful, but only those whose names are written in the Lamb's book of life (Revelation 21:24–27 NIV).

There are several key characteristics of this new culture that John establishes in this passage:

A citizenship of mercy — As the vast pan-national family of God, we will love one another perfectly. We will walk together by the light of God's glory, for each of us will *never* forget that our passport into the new heaven and new earth was the Lamb's book of life, which proclaimed His death as ours. We will always love much, because we have been forgiven and healed of *everything*.

An economy of grace — Imagine what it will be like when the riches of the nations and the wealth of kings are surrendered to the benevolent and wise King of the ages. Never again will there be a problem of unfair distribution. We will never love money again, just one another as neighbors. Overspeculation about the economy in the New Jerusalem is unwarranted, but of this we can be sure: it will *always* be a testimony to the grace and generosity of Jesus.

A society of justice — Because deceit and impurity will never infiltrate the New Jerusalem, as was the case in the Garden of Eden, a culture of justice and righteousness will eternally prevail throughout the new heaven and new earth. Never again will there be oppression, exploitation, poverty, slavery, hunger, thirst, or homelessness.

A technology of peace — With kings and nations no longer having greed, anger, or war in their hearts, then swords, spears, battleships, and bombers will all be smelted into things useful for a technology and culture of shalom. What is the future of inventiveness? I cannot wait to find out.

A global art colony of glory — Among the innumerable artifacts of splendor, glory, and honor brought into the New Jerusalem, surely there will be noble and notable expressions of artwork created on the journey between the Garden of Eden and the New Jerusalem. I'm not suggesting helicopters will land and unload crates from The Louvre; but, in ways we simply cannot fathom, the history of art will be celebrated and redeemed. Just think of what it will be like to live in a world of redeemed artists—from every people group throughout the history of redemption—whose hearts are devoid of all sin and whose vision of God's glory is undiluted.

A politic of servanthood — Oh, for the day when the redeemed kings of the world will join the healed nations from history and reign together, forever, in the new heaven and new earth as *worship servants*! Then, we will know the consummate joy of humility and the everlasting beauty of thinking of others more highly than ourselves.

An educational environment of wonder —We will continue to learn, not to prepare for exams, but to create new culture for the sake of exalting our God forever.

CULTURE MAKING TODAY

What, then, does obedience to the cultural mandate look like for us today? How can we help restore broken culture and build redemptive culture en route to the New Jerusalem? David Hegeman makes a strong case for using the construction of Israel's tabernacle and temple as a paradigm for our never-ending calling to make culture to the glory of God—in this world and the next.

> The variety of occupations used in the building of the tabernacle and temple is astounding: lumbermen, carpenters, spinners, dyers, weavers, embroiderers, seamstresses, foundry workers and metallurgists, goldsmiths, engravers, jewelers, tanners, perfumers, quarry workers, and stone masons.
>
> Then there were those who provided direct logistical support: tool makers, keepers of draft animals, seafarers, and laborers. In addition to the craftsmen and laborers, there were those who were involved in the worship activities after the sanctuaries were completed: priests and attendants, musicians, singers, musical instrument makers and psalmists.
>
> The gracious circumstances of OT redemption are a resounding celebration of vocational diversity and human skill. The tabernacle and temple were both emblematic—on a small scale—of the grand diversity which was to mark the global culturative endeavor given to man in the Garden of Eden. And they point forward to the wondrous culturative potentialities which will be released after the consummation, when a glorified, sinless humanity fulfills with perfection the culturative development of the new earth.[3]

The multiple occupations and skills utilized in building both the tabernacle and the temple are indicative of the fertile cultural seed God sowed in the Garden of Eden. These vocations, endowments, and abilities—and a plethora of others—are expressions of the ongoing viability of the cultural mandate. Every one of these occupations is a gift of God, precious to Him. God was pleased and praised the faithful exercise of these skills and talents before they were ever employed in the construction of the tabernacle or temple.

The carpenter's woodwork in the temple wasn't more sacred than the table he built for his wife, or the repairs he made on a neighbor's home. The embroiderer's handiwork hanging in the tabernacle didn't proclaim God's glory any louder than the well-made pillow she sold in the market. To use an example from today, Steven Curtis's voice is just as pleasing to Jesus when he is singing a love song to Mary Beth or jamming with his sons' garage band as when he is singing to 30,000 people at a Billy Graham Crusade.

Though the Fall *corrupted*, it could never *cancel* our culturative calling. Though sin has perverted our motives and changed the goal, the call to make culture was given before the Fall, and it will continue after Jesus has made all things new.

This is the bottom line: we are to offer God *worship service* wherever He has placed us, and in whatever we are doing. Whether we are singing praise songs in a service of worship, playing checkers with our children, fishing for Brown Speckled Trout in Montana, roofing the home of an elderly widow across town, or working hard in our vocation. The apostle Paul summarized the cultural mandate with this admonition to believers in Corinth: "So whether you eat or drink or whatever you do, do it all for the glory of God" (1 Corinthians 10:31 NIV).

Through the centuries, the church has minimized, idolized, spiritualized, and demonized our calling to be *in the world* (making godly culture), but not *of the world* (being squeezed into the world's mold). However, the leaders of the Reformation are remembered for helping believers faithfully live as citizens of two kingdoms: the kingdom of this world and the kingdom of God. Michael Scott Horton writes:

> The reformers avoided (two) tendencies: on the one hand, to confuse the two kingdoms (Rome's mistake) and, on the other, to divorce the two kingdoms and reject any Christian involvement in the kingdom of culture (Anabaptist's mistake). Instead, they insisted that Christians should be involved in the world. They should neither seek to escape it, like the monks, whose lives were often more "worldly" than the world, nor seek to rule it, like the popes, whose own houses were not quite in order.
>
> Every believer is a "priest" before God, and each person (believer and unbeliever) has been given a vocation of calling, by virtue of creation, to participate in some way in culture. We are social beings, created to enjoy each other's company, whether Christian or non-Christian. Redemption does not change our participation in culture; rather, it changes us and therefore, the character of our involvement.
>
> Separation from the world is not physical, according to the reformers; rather, it is a matter of divorcing our dependence on the things of this world; its vanity and rejection or perversion of things heavenly. Luther and Calvin said that the calling of the magistrate or public official was "one of the noblest" (Calvin), inasmuch as it serves the society well.[4]

FOR FURTHER REFLECTION

How has this chapter led you to think differently about culture and the cultural mandate?

Looking ahead to the culture making of the new heaven and new earth, what thrills you? What questions have been generated by the very idea of eternal culture making?

What is your sense of vocation? How would you define your calling?

What appeals to you more: "ministry," or working in the culture? How would you distinguish the two?

How is God praised by excellence? Define excellence. What is the difference between excellent culture and cultural elitism?

Who or what has shaped your aesthetic of beauty? Describe a beautiful person.

Ruling, working, filling, and keeping . . . how can you presently and intentionally engage in each of these to the glory of God?

What creative enterprise or hobby have you always wanted to try, but, for various reasons, have begged off? Why not risk a new adventure in creativity in the next three months.

If you could be an artist, what medium would you choose?

Where can you bring the firstfruits of the good, the true, and the beautiful? Think of several areas in which you are uniquely placed by God to bring beauty.

Conclusion: What on Earth Are We Doing?

"Heaven on earth, we need it now . . .
I'm sick of all of this hanging around
Sick of sorrow, sick of the pain
I'm sick of hearing again and again that there's gonna be
peace on earth"
— U2, "Peace on Earth"

"We read the gospel as if we had no money, and we spend our money
as if we know nothing of the gospel."
— John Haughey

"If this should be my last day on this earth how then shall I live?
Oh, if this should be the last day that I have . . .
before I breathe the air of Heaven,
Let me live it with abandon to the only One that remains"
— SCC, "Last Day on Earth"

(Steven):

Fifteen grief-stricken women filled the little green tent donated by German Christians. Each was given an opportunity to share their heartbreaking story. Though I regularly care for children and families in great crisis, *nothing* could have prepared me for what I was about to hear.

"The first time I heard, 'I was holding onto both of my children, and I couldn't hold on anymore. I had to let one of them go . . .' The first time I heard, 'My sister, my mother . . . they ran and tried to climb the barbwire fence, only to have their saris and hair get caught in the fence and they drowned.' The first time I saw actual photos of the children who were taken to sea . . . I was undone.

"As I sat there surrounded by people I didn't know who were sharing their most intimate grief, I felt my heart break. I had not known grief like that before. I had not wept in front of complete strangers like I did in that tent on February 2, 2005. I am not sure how long I sobbed, but when I looked up, our translator, Rovi, and many of the women were crying. Rovi shared with me that the women said I was the first foreigner who had cried for them and had not just dropped food off and left."

These are the words and heart of our dear friend, Sharon Dale, a gifted counselor in our church and community. She shared this report with our congregation just after returning from Sri Lanka, where we sent Sharon to help with the enormous need for post-trauma caregiving and counseling. When the history-shaping tragedy of the south Asian tsunami took place on December 26, 2004, Sharon was the first of many of our members from Christ Community sent to the areas most devastated by the tsunami. We went to extend the tear-wiping hand of God, and to offer whatever assistance we could.

The incalculable destruction created by this single catastrophe has indelibly underscored the central theme of our book: every

Christian is called to engage with Jesus' commitment to make all things new. Each of us is privileged and called to become a *character in* and *carrier of* God's Story of redemption and restoration through Jesus. The tsunami has proven to be a megaphone by which the mega-needs of our broken world have been loudly broadcast. The essentiality of Jesus' redeeming love and renewing power has once again been clearly revealed.

By the time this book goes to press, it is estimated that nearly 300,000 people will have lost their lives and five million will have been left homeless by the tsunami. The entire population and all physical structures of some villages simply disappeared. Some pastors never got to bury even one of their parishioners, as the membership of whole congregations were swept out to sea. It will take *many* years to rebuild the physical, economic, and social infrastructure within the areas most severely affected by the tsunami.

This crisis brought profound significance and prophetic urgency to the underlying message of this book. How are we to understand such devastation? Why do these kinds of things happen? Where was Jesus when the earth began to quake at the bottom of the ocean? Who is going to care for all these people in the aftermath of such great loss, and in view of the "present math" estimates of the cost of restoration? Indeed, *what* on earth is Jesus doing?

This searching question finds its answer in another question— one perhaps even more searching and certainly more disruptive. What on earth are *we* doing in Jesus' name? A story recorded in the Gospel of Mark demonstrates how these two questions, and their answers, are vitally related to one another.

Late one afternoon, Jesus' disciples faced the mounting hunger pangs of a crowd of as many as 10,000 men, women, and children who had gathered to listen to the Good Shepherd teach (Mark 6:30–44). This open-air assembly had taken place in a remote place that was a considerable walking distance from an ample food supply. With compassion for the masses, the disciples encouraged Jesus to "send them away to go into the surrounding countryside and villages and buy themselves something to eat" (v. 36).

Oh, to have seen the look on the disciples' faces when Jesus turned and said to them, "*You* give them something to eat. Yeah, why don't you guys pool your picnics and feed them. What do you have in your backpacks?"

"Well, let's see . . . we've got five loaves and two fish between us—obviously not enough to feed this many people, Jesus. It'd take eight months of a man's salary to feed this many people." But as the story unfolds, the disciples' bewilderment gave way to astonishment as Jesus took their love offering, gave thanks to the Father, and fed the enormous crowd. And after everyone had their fill, twelve baskets full of bread and fish were gathered as leftovers—enough to feed *many more* hungry people.

Was this a miracle? *Of course it was.* But it was much more than a *mere* miracle. It was also a clear message about *what* on earth Jesus is doing, and a revelation of *how* He delights to accomplish His will. Jesus takes insufficient people with inadequate resources into impossible situations to reveal the wonders of His grace and the presence of His kingdom. He is calling *us*, indeed the whole body of Christ, into a life of *worship service*—a life of doxological mission and mercy. *We* are the means by which His compassionate and generous heart is to be manifest in the broken places. *We* are to be the extension of Jesus' healing, tear-wiping hands, in offering living hope and the firstfruits of the day when there will be no more death, mourning, pain, and hunger.

By *this* kind of love and service, we loudly proclaim Jesus' defeat of Satan and the powers of darkness. And, little by little, we push back the effects of the Fall. By *this* kind of generosity and engagement, we demonstrate the irrefutable arrival of Jesus' restoring and redeeming kingdom.

What on earth *are* we doing in Jesus' name? What on earth are *you* doing with the grace of Jesus lavished upon you so freely? If this should be our last day, last month, or last year on earth, how shall we live? These aren't questions of guilt, but of love. The issue before us isn't one of performance and earning God's favor, but praise and revealing God's glory. There's no condemnation toward us in Christ, but there certainly *must* be conviction by the Holy Spirit!

The first Sunday after the mind-numbing tsunami hit, Scotty preached a sermon from a difficult season in the apostle Paul's life. In fact, it involved a personal crisis in Asia and a devastating famine in Judea. Scotty's words helped our church family put the tragedy of the tsunami—and suffering in general—into perspective. And he challenged us to find our place of response as a body of believers. I'll let Scotty share what God taught us that morning.

WHY THESE THINGS HAPPEN:

Reflections on the Asian Crisis, Suffering, and the Purposes of God
(2 Corinthians 1:1–11; 8:1–9; 9:6–15)

(Scotty:)

As we remain stunned in the aftermath and the inconceivable devastation from the Asian tsunami, how can we possibly know what to feel? How do we make sense of such a tragic event and the incalculable suffering? The gospel frees us from all pretending and trying to put an acceptable spin on this story. We're not supposed to *like* these kinds of things. We're not supposed to reach for a spiritual band-aid or easy answer. While God certainly works all things for good of those who love him (Romans 8:28), some things in and of themselves *are not good*. Period. Thankfully, Jesus calls us and frees us to engage with, not escape from, the overwhelming tragedies and the great sufferings of life.

Paul knew firsthand about tragedies. His second letter to the Corinthians is filled with the pathos and passion of a believer personally familiar with great pain and loss, and is *captured* with the heart and ways of Jesus. Second Corinthians was written with a rawness and reality that reveal both authentic struggle and a very present Savior.

As I enter Paul's story, I am reminded, encouraged, and convicted to see how he responded to difficult questions about suffering and the crises we experience in life as followers of Jesus— just like the ones before us now. Here's the first thing that strikes me: when confronted with confusing, even biting, questions about his own suffering and great suffering in the world, Paul didn't offer *philosophical explanations,* but *teleological reasons.* Let me explain.

In essence, a life shaped by *teleology* is a life lived along a story line—a life lived with a view to the future. The Greek word *teleos* means "end" or "goal." When used in the context of biblical faith and our relationship with Jesus, it presupposes that *history* has meaning and *people* have meaning, and that *all things* are to be understood in light of God's ultimate purposes revealed in Jesus.

Though Paul was a profoundly gifted scholar and philosopher, who could give well-reasoned and impressive answers to difficult queries, he chose to respond to the Corinthians not in terms of intellectual notions, but in terms of redemptive narrative. By doing this, Paul modeled the important difference between asking the self-centered question, "Why me, Lord?" versus asking the God-centered question, "What now, Lord?"

Basically, it's the difference between expecting "because" answers to difficult questions versus looking for "so that" answers to difficult events. "Because" answers focus on giving a good reason; "so that" answers are more concerned about giving a godly response. So how does this translate into real life?

Consider Paul's opening words to believers in Corinth, and notice how he addresses the issues of suffering and hardship. Note how he writes with a refreshing honesty and vulnerability about his own personal crisis in Asia.

Blessed be the God and Father of our Lord Jesus Christ, the Father of mercies and God of all comfort, who comforts us in all our affliction, *so that* we may be able to comfort those who are in any affliction, with the comfort with which we ourselves are comforted by God. For as we share abundantly in Christ's sufferings, so through Christ we share abundantly in comfort too. If we are afflicted, it is for your comfort and salvation; and if we are comforted, it is for your comfort, which you experience when you patiently endure the same sufferings that we suffer. Our hope for you is unshaken, for we know that as you share in our sufferings, you will also share in our comfort. For we do not want you to be ignorant, brothers, of the affliction we experienced in Asia. For we were so utterly burdened beyond our strength that we despaired of life itself. Indeed, we felt that we had received the sentence of death. But that was to make us rely not on ourselves but on God who raises the dead. He delivered us from such a deadly peril, and he will deliver us. On him we have set our hope that he will deliver us again. You also must help us by prayer, *so that* many will give thanks on our behalf for the blessing granted us through the prayers of many (2 Corinthians 1:3–11, emphasis mine).

"So That" Living

In 2 Corinthians, Paul deals with a series of challenging questions that emerge within the storyline of the letter. By reading 1 and 2 Corinthians together, we can reconstruct many of these questions to which the apostle was responding. There is one important part of the story behind the writing of this letter that is worth noting.

There was a significant famine underway in Judea as Paul wrote 2 Corinthians. Jewish Christians were in desperate need of help, and Paul had taken responsibility for collecting a famine relief fund from the Gentile churches to provide this relief. Initially, the Corinthian believers responded to Paul's call for help; but their enthusiasm, along with their generosity, was waning. He is writing to reconnect the Corinthian church with their missional calling. Keep this part of the story in mind as we study the apostle's answers to important questions.

- **Paul, why did you suffer so greatly in Asia?** (2 Corinthians 1:8–10)

Instead of offering a *"because"* answer to this important question such as, "This happened because we didn't have enough faith;" or "because we live in a fallen world;" or "because our obedience was incomplete," Paul gave a "so that" response. "This happened *that* we might not rely on ourselves but on God, who raises the dead" (2 Corinthians 1:9 NIV, emphasis mine).

What an amazing response! In essence, here's what Paul was saying: "Why did I suffer in Asia? *So that* I might more fully enter into God's Story of making all things new. Through Jesus' death and resurrection, God is bringing life to dead things and dead people. Though I am tempted to live life as a self-centered, self-sufficient man, God has called me—and you—into a greater story. God will always bring us to the end of ourselves *so that* we might rely upon Jesus and identify more fully with his purposes and passions."

- **Paul, if Jesus already suffered for us, why do we continue to suffer so much in life?** (2 Corinthians 1:3–7)

"We suffer with Christ abundantly in this broken world and are comforted by our merciful Father *so that* we might be better equipped to enter into the sufferings of others and comfort them with the very comfort God brings us through Jesus.

"Jesus didn't die so that we would escape suffering in this world, but to eliminate suffering in the world to come. He is preparing us to enter in more fully to the sufferings of others, *so that* we might share the gospel with them and bring His restorative mercy and grace to their broken situation."

- **Paul, if we're going to suffer abundantly, why pray? What good will it do?** (2 Corinthians 1:11)

"God did not give us prayer as a pragmatic tool for getting our way, but as a providential means of revealing His glory. Therefore, 'You also must help us by prayer, *so that* many will give thanks on our behalf for the blessing granted us through the prayers of many' (emphasis mine). Prayer will expand our hearts to the greater good God is up to, which always includes more people than us."

- **Paul, why did God allow the horrible famine in Judea?** (2 Corinthians 9:12–13)

"This happened *so that* God might bring glory to Himself as Gentile believers respond compassionately and sacrificially to the needs of Jewish believers. The world will marvel at this miracle of servanthood and cross-cultural mercy, and God will be greatly praised.

"'For the ministry of this service is not only supplying the needs of the saints, but is also overflowing in many thanksgivings to God. By their [Jewish believers'] approval of this service, they will glorify God because of your [Gentile believers'] submission flowing from your confession of the gospel of Christ, and the generosity of your contribution for them and for all others.'"

- **Paul, why does God bless us so abundantly in life?**
  (2 Corinthians 9:8–9)

"This happened *so that* we may be content and abound in the good works of generosity to the poor. 'And God is able to provide you with every blessing in abundance, so that having all contentment in all things at all times, you may abound in every good work. As it is written, "He has distributed freely, he has given to the poor; his righteousness endures forever." ' "

- **Paul, why did Jesus embrace the poverty of his incarnation?**
  (2 Corinthians 8:9)

"This happened *so that* by his poverty you may become rich, and like him, become a cheerful giver, enriching others. 'For you know the grace of our Lord Jesus Christ, that though he was rich, yet for your sake he became poor, *so that* you by his poverty might become rich' " (emphasis mine).

WHY WAS THERE A TSUNAMI IN ASIA?

(STEVEN:)

Scotty and I would like to offer a *so that* answer to that question: *so that* we'd live every day as though we were in the season of Advent. In God's Story, Advent is a time of anticipation and of preparation—a getting ready for the two-stage arrival of the promised Messiah. Christmas is a celebration of the *first* Advent of Jesus, but it is also a reminder of His *second* Advent, the day when Jesus will return to receive His Bride and usher in the new heaven and new earth.

Consider the significance of the date of the tsunami—December 26, 2004—the day immediately following our annual celebration of Jesus' birth. What is Christmas all about? Why did Jesus come into this world? On the first day of His public ministry, Jesus left no doubt about His identity and His destiny.

And he came to Nazareth, where he had been brought up. And as was his custom, he went to the synagogue on the Sabbath day, and he stood up to read. And the scroll of the prophet Isaiah was given to him. He unrolled the scroll and found the place where it was written, "The Spirit of the Lord is upon me, because he has anointed me to proclaim good news to the poor. He has sent me to proclaim liberty to the captives and recovering of sight to the blind, to set at liberty those who are oppressed, to proclaim the year of the Lord's favor." And he rolled up the scroll and gave it back to the attendant and sat down. And the eyes of all in the synagogue were fixed on him. And he began to say to them, "Today this Scripture has been fulfilled in your hearing" (Luke 4:16–21).

"Bodaciously," as people say in North Carolina, Jesus claimed to be the One about whom Isaiah was writing. Without hesitation or equivocation, Jesus announced, "Christmas is here. The last days have just begun! Isaiah's every hope and dream and the promises of all the other prophets are met in the One standing before you. You won't be harvesting sin and sorrows much longer. Thorns will soon stop infesting the ground and your gardens. I've come to make My blessings flow as far as the curse of sin and death can be found! I already rule this world, *My* world, with truth and grace. And in time, I'll make the nations—*all* of them, not just Israel—prove the glories of My righteousness and the wonders of *My* love. Merry Christmas everyone!"

What on Earth Is Jesus Doing?

As soon as that synagogue service was over, Jesus began confirming His bold claim to be the Messiah. Consider the following chronicle of Jesus' unfolding ministry activity recorded by Luke. What on earth is Jesus doing?

Luke 4:31ff. — Jesus frees a demonized man. He has authority over all evil, all the powers of darkness, including the kingdom of Satan.

Luke 4:38ff. — Jesus heals Peter's mother-in-law, heals those with "various diseases," and releases many more broken people from their demonic bondage.

Luke 4:42ff. — Jesus announces the good news and arrival of the kingdom of God, and He begins to proclaim this news in the synagogues of Judea.

Luke 5:12ff. — Jesus heals a leper—the AIDS sufferer of His day. Leprosy devastated a person's life—socially, physically, emotionally, mentally, spiritually, and economically. Jesus cares about every aspect of our humanity and culture.

Luke 5:17ff. — Jesus heals a paralytic, indicative of the literal and metaphorical ways we are paralyzed and bound by the consequences of sin and death.

Luke 5:33 — Jesus confronts the old wineskins of nationalistic religion with the new wine of His kingdom.

Luke 7:1ff. — Jesus heals a Roman centurion's servant. He brings "good news for *all* the people," even despised Roman officials.

Luke 7:11ff. — Jesus raises a young man from the dead. He has power over death and He alone can give life, for He is the resurrection and the life!

Luke 7:22–23 — Jesus responds to John the Baptist's doubts about His identity. In a touching scene, we notice that followers of Jesus are sometimes weak and have doubts, but Jesus extends compassion and grace to us, just as He did to John the Baptist. "Go and tell John what you have seen and heard: the blind receive their sight, the lame walk, lepers are cleansed, and the deaf hear, the dead are raised up, the poor have good news preached to them. And blessed is the one who is not offended by me."

Luke 7:36ff. — Jesus receives adoration from a "sinful" woman in the home of a Pharisee. Jesus exposes the sinfulness of self-righteousness and befriends sinners, including whores, the demonized, and the marginalized.

Luke 8:1ff. — Jesus welcomes women as His followers, including Mary Magdalene, whom He freed from seven demons, and Joanna, who was the wife of Herod's household manager. Jesus confronts the cultural bias and inequities marshaled toward women in His day.

Luke 8:22ff. — Jesus calms a storm. He has authority over nature. He created the cosmos and sustains every atom by the power of His word. His love, care, and kingdom are extended to creation, and not just to the world's citizens.

Luke 9:10ff. — Jesus feeds 5,000 people—physically and spiritually. He confronts hunger on every front. He brings good news, but also bread, to the poor.

Luke 10:25ff. — Jesus tells the parable of the Good Samaritan: a story of international grace and local mercy. Israel had never put the words *good* and *Samaritan* together before Christ the Liberator showed up. The Samaritan is celebrated as a model of true piety. If our participation in *services of worship* does not result in *worship service*, then what we call worship is nothing more than naval-gazing idolatry, religious recreation, or societal pageantry.

Luke 11:42 — Jesus confronts the arrogance and lovelessness of Pharisaical religion. "But woe to you Pharisees! For you tithe mint and rue and every herb, and neglect justice and the love of God. These you ought to have done, without neglecting the others." Jesus fulfills the law for us, and in us, so that He can fill us with the grace of generosity.

restoring broken things

Practicing for the New Life

Luke's Gospel shows us clearly what Jesus was doing on earth during His first Advent, and John's visions in Revelation show the work Jesus will complete at His second Advent. Therefore, as followers of Jesus, doesn't it stand to reason that we are called to practice, in the present time, the social conditions that anticipate the society we will enjoy forever in the new heaven and new earth?

This is how we are to live between the advents of Jesus. This is what it means to pray, "Jesus, may your kingdom come and your will be done, on earth as it is in heaven." We are to bring the Word and work of Jesus to every nation and neighborhood: by proclaiming the gospel of His saving grace, and by breaking the oppressive yokes of injustice as we pour ourselves out for the broken. The tsunami is a crisis . . . as is AIDS, idolatry, orphans, legalism, poverty, injustice, self-righteousness, sin, and death . . . for which Jesus alone is the answer.

How then are we to live on earth to the glory of God? What will living as true worshipers require of us? Among many good suggestions, Scotty and I want to offer one of the most basic, simple, and tangible ways *all* of us can participate in Jesus' commitment to make all things new. It begins with reexamining our relationship with money—what we earn and what we are given. To be specific, what would keep *any* of us from setting aside at *least* 10 percent of whatever monies we receive for the things about which Jesus is passionate? What possible reason could we give for *not* choosing to do so? This isn't legalism—it's love.

Jesus talked a great deal about money. In fact, sixteen of his thirty-eight parables are concerned with how people handle money

246

and possessions. In the Gospels, one out of ten verses deal directly with the issue of money. The Bible, as a whole, presents five hundred verses on prayer and less than five hundred verses on faith, but more than two thousand verses on money and possessions. If followers of Jesus in the Roman world of the first century proclaimed, "Jesus is Lord, and Caesar is not!" then followers of Jesus in America of the twenty-first century need to proclaim, "Jesus is Lord, and money is not!"

We need markers to remind us of our participation in God's story of liberation and generosity. Baptism and the Lord's Supper are the two main markers we have been given. But on a weekly basis, presenting tithes and love offerings to the Lord serves as a powerful reminder and participation in this story.

To tithe is to affirm with joy: "I am not my own. Everything I have and am belongs to Jesus, who, by His grace, has completely paid the debt I owe God. He has brought me into the freedom and inheritance of the sons of God, and has called me to live as a tenant in His world. I am simply a steward of His resources, and an agent of His mercy, justice, and peace. What an honor and privilege!"

Consider the following: Americans spent 217 *billion* dollars on Christmas gifts, decorations, and parties in 2003. Yet, in Africa, the World Trade Center falls twice a day as 6500 men, women, and children die of AIDS *daily*. There are 13 million AIDS orphans under the age of fifteen, and this number will reach 40 million by 2010. An estimated 200 million people go to bed hungry every night in sub-Saharan Africa.

In 1933, when the Great Depression was at its worst, the average church member gave 3.3 percent of his income. By 2000, after fifty years of great prosperity, the average church member gave 2.6 percent. If members of historically Christian churches in America had given 10 percent of their incomes in 2000, an additional $139 billion could have been invested in ministries of the gospel and caring for the poor.

Is there any doubt, then, about why we say that getting serious about loving Jesus will always involve getting serious about what we do with money?

How Then Shall We Live?
By Making Much of Jesus

"I want to make much of You, Jesus,
I want to make much of Your love
I want to live today to give You the praise
that You alone are so worthy of
I want to make much of Your mercy,
I want to make much of Your cross
I give You my life ... take it and let it be used to
make much of You"
— SCC, "Much of You"

Jesus is the Advocate we all desperately long for. He's the powerful Liberator who comes to destroy captivities, injustice, oppression, inequities, hoarding, nationalism, dysfunction, disease, hunger, abuse, racism, demonic strongholds, systemic evil, and every form of hating and harming. What other story is worthy of the rest of our lives, tears, money, passion, strength, and everything else we have and are?

Joy to the world, the Lord has come—and is coming again! Let earth receive her King! Let us, therefore, give Him the *worship service* He deserves, and in which He delights.

By Loving Sacrificially

By this we know love, that he laid down his life for us, and we ought to lay down our lives for the brothers. But if anyone has the world's goods and sees his brother in need, yet closes his heart against him, how does God's love abide in him? Little children, let us not love in word or talk but in deed and in truth (1 John 3:16–18).

By Living Contentedly

Now there is great gain in godliness with contentment, for we brought nothing into the world, and we cannot take anything out of the world. But if we have food and clothing, with these we will be content. But those who desire to be rich fall into temptation, into a snare, into many senseless and harmful desires that plunge people into ruin and destruction. For the love of money is a root of all kinds of evils. It is through this craving that some have wandered away from the faith and pierced themselves with many pangs (1 Timothy 6:6–10).

By Loving Generously

As for the rich in this present age, charge them not to be haughty, nor to set their hopes on the uncertainty of riches, but on God, who richly provides us with everything to enjoy. They are to do good, to be rich in good works, to be generous and ready to share, thus storing up treasure for themselves as a good foundation for the future, so that they may take hold of that which is truly life (1 Timothy 6:17–19).

By Longing Expectantly
Then the angel showed me the river of the water of life, as clear as crystal, flowing from the throne of God and of the Lamb down the middle of the great street of the city. On each side of the river stood the tree of life, bearing twelve crops of fruit, yielding its fruit every month. And the leaves of the tree are for the healing of the nations. No longer will there be any curse. The throne of God and of the Lamb will be in the city, and his servants will serve him. They will see his face, and his name will be on their foreheads. There will be no more night. They will not need the light of a lamp or the light of the sun, for the Lord God will give them light. And they will reign for ever and ever (Revelation 22:1–5 NIV).

For the day is coming, and may it be soon, when the story of redemption will give way to the glory of consummation. On that day of cosmic transformation, we will *finally* be freed to celebrate our eternal vocation of serving God as an eternal vacation of enjoying God! Oh, to be so liberated and joyful! No one has captured the essence of this coming wonder-world better than C. S. Lewis:

> "There was a real railway accident," said Aslan softly. "Your father and mother and all of you are—as you used to call it in the Shadow-Lands—dead. The term is over; the holidays have begun. The dream is ended: this is the morning.

"And as he spoke he no longer looked to them like a lion; but the things that began to happen after that were so great and beautiful that I cannot write them. And for us this is the end of all the stories, and we can most truly say that they all lived happily ever after. But for them it was only the beginning of the real story. All their life in this world and all their adventures in Narnia had only been the cover and the title page: now at last they were beginning Chapter One of the Great Story, which no one on earth had read: which goes on for ever: in which every chapter is better than the one before."[1]

Let's do everything in our power to live the rest of the "cover and title page" in the one "Great Story" to the glory of the One who is making all things new, Jesus. Hallelujah! What a salvation! Hallelujah! What a Savior!

ENDNOTES

Chapter 1

1. N. T. Wright, *Following Jesus* (Grand Rapids: William B. Eerdman's Publishing Co., 1994), 54.

2. Craig VanGelder, *The Essence of the Church* (Grand Rapids: Baker Books, 2000), 89–90.

Chapter 2

1. John Eldredge, *Epic* (Nashville: Thomas Nelson, 2004), 2–3.

2. Henri J. M. Nouwen, *The Return of the Prodigal Son* (New York: Doubleday, 1994), 103.

3. Paul Ford, *Companion to Narnia* (San Francisco: Harper & Row, 1983), xiv.

4. N. T. Wright, *The Millennium Myth* (Louisville: Westminster John Knox Press, 1999), 54–55.

5. R. Paul Stevens and M. Green, *The Living Story* (Grand Rapids: William B. Eerdman's Publishing Co., 2003), ix.

Chapter 3

1. Anne Lamott, *Traveling Mercies* (New York: Anchor Books, 2000), 100.

2. Graeme Goldworthy, "The Gospel in Revelation," *The Goldsworthy Trilogy* (Waynesboro: Pasternoster Press, 2000), 315.

3. Philip E. Hughes, *The Book of Revelation* (England: InterVarsity Press, 1990), 10–11.

Chapter 5

1. Wayne Martindale and J. Root, ed., *The Quotable Lewis* (Wheaton: Tyndale House, 1989), 134.

2. Albert M. Wolters, *Creation Regained* (Grand Rapids: Williams B. Eerdman's Publishing Co., 1998), 69–70.

Endnotes

Chapter 6

1. Tim Keller, *Romans: A Study Course in the Gospel* (v. 2.0), (New York: Redeemer Presbyterian Church, 1997), D9–10.

Chapter 9

1. Michael Wilcock, *I Saw Heaven Opened* (Downers Grove: InterVarsity Press, 1975), 22.

Chapter 10

1. Eugene Peterson, *Reversed Thunder* (San Francisco: Harper Collins, 1991), 174, 183.

Chapter 11

1. David Bruce Hegeman, *Plowing in Hope* (Moscow: Canon Press, 1991), 35, 42–46.

2. Richard Mouw, *When the Kings Come Marching In* (Grand Rapids: William Eerdman's Publishing Co., 1983), 64–65.

3. Hegeman, David Bruce. *Plowing in Hope* (Moscow: Canon Press, 1991), 35, 42–46.

4. Michael Scott Horton, *Beyond Culture Wars* (Chicago: Moody Publications, 1994), 180.

Conclusion:

1. C. S. Lewis, *The Last Battle* (New York: Collier-Macmillan, 1970).